DINNER IS SERVED

DINNER IS SERVED

A History of Dining in England
1400-1900

Gerard Brett

1968
Rupert Hart-Davis

Produced by Design Yearbook Limited, 21 Ivor Place, London N.W.1.
Published by Rupert Hart-Davis Limited, 1 Upper James Street, London W.1.
Text set by J. M. Clarke Limited, 20 Vittoria Street, Birmingham 1.
Printed by Compton Printing Limited, Pembroke Road, Stocklake, Aylesbury, Bucks.
Bound by William Brendon and Son Limited, Tiptree, Essex.
© *Gerard Brett* 1968

Designed by Jacque Solomons

First published 1968.

Printed in England.

SBN: 246.64469.9

Contents

IIIustrations

the 1880 edition of *Mrs. Beeton*. **Page 117**

Plate 53 Set of three Casters, silver. Ht. 6¼″. London, 1736, by Samuel Wood. London, Victoria and Albert Museum. Crown Copyright Reserved. **Page 119**

Plate 54 Cruet Stand, silver. Ht. 8½″. London, 1760, by John Dalmester. Toronto, Royal Ontario Museum. **Page 120**

Plate 55 Cruet Stands. Left, silver with silver-mounted glass bottles and containers for oil, vinegar, sugar, salt, pepper and mustard. Ht. 9½″. London, 1831, by R. Hennell. Toronto, Royal Ontario Museum. Right, silver with silver-stoppered glass bottles for oil and vinegar and silver casters for salt, pepper and ? sugar. Ht. 10½″. London, 1753-4, by Samuel Wells. Toronto, private possession. **Page 121**

Plate 56 Decanters, the smaller one wheel-engraved with a pen and a rose for George and William Penrose. Hts. 9¾″, 11⅛″. The larger English, 3rd quarter 18th century, the smaller Irish, late 18th century. Toronto, Royal Ontario Museum. **Page 123**

Plate 57 Decanter, glass. Ht. 10¼″. English or Irish, late 18th or early 19th century. Toronto, Royal Ontario Museum. **Page 124**

Plate 58 Decanter, clear and coated glass. Ht. 11½″. English, 19th century. Toronto, Royal Ontario Museum. **Page 127**

Plate 59 Flagons, silver. Ht. 15½″. Edinburgh, 1835, by J. McKay. Toronto, Royal Ontario Museum. **Page 128**

Plate 60 Flint glass. Ht. 8⅞″. English, 1690-1700. Toronto, Royal Ontario Museum. **Page 130**

Plate 61 Air-twist and enamel-twist glasses, the latter with a wheel-engraved portrait and the inscription 'George Prince of Wales, 1759'. Toronto, Royal Ontario Museum. **Page 131**

Plate 62 One from a set of twelve finger bowls, glass. Ht. 4″. English or Irish, 1820-30. Toronto, private possession. **Page 132**

Plate 63 Caddinet, silver-gilt. 14¾″ x 12″. One of a pair hallmarked respectively 1683-4 and 1688-9; the latter by Antony Nelme. On loan to the Victoria and Albert Museum from the Earl of Lonsdale. **Page 133**

Preface

This book is concerned with the setting, arrangements and customs of the English dinner table during the years from about 1400—1900. It deals in part with food, in part with the vessels, the implements of eating, and the drinking cups in use at different times.

The book is divided into two parts, Medieval and Modern, at the Restoration in 1660. By the standards of political and of economic history this date is of course too late; but social history has an independent time scale of its own. The table fork, the typical implement of the modern period makes its appearance in England in the later sixteenth century; the latest written text to describe the medieval manner of eating as a living whole, dates from the first part of the seventeenth century. The seventy or eighty years between these two events are an interim stage in which the two manners of eating exist side by side: 1660 is a significant date which can conveniently be used to mark its end, though it is likely that the change took at least another fifty years.

Something must also be said about the general character of this book. The subject is not by any means a new one, but those who have treated it in recent years have often written in what one of the later editors of Mrs. Beeton calls a 'cosy, chatty' tone, which is becoming inseparable from the subject. I feel, on the other hand, that it is important enough to deserve a different handling, and if what I have written sometimes seems almost cold and unemotional, I must ask the reader to accept this as my reason.

Many people have helped me in writing, most of them by lending books in their own possession. To try and mention all the names, if it were possible, would result in a list of a length quite disproportionate to that of the book itself, and I must therefore ask those involved to accept my sincere and most grateful thanks. Four names only I must mention — my wife, of whom the old and now much abused *cliché* is literally true, that without her constant help and encouragement this book would never have been written; my former secretary Mary Campbell, my friend Dr. Naomi Groves and my brother Lionel. All these have made many useful suggestions, and the book owes much to them.

I must also offer sincere thanks to the Chief Librarian and many staff members of the University Library, University of Toronto.

Gerard Brett
1967

Introduction

'At meat her manners were well taught withal;
No morsel from her lips did she let fall
Nor dipped her fingers in the sauce too deep;
But she could carry a morsel up and keep
The smallest drop from falling on her breast.
For courtliness she had a special zest.
And she would wipe her upper lip so clean
That not a trace of grease was to be seen
Upon the cup when she had drunk; to eat
She reached a hand sedately for the meat . . .'*

*Chaucer, *Canterbury Tales*, ed. Neville Coghill (London, Penguin Books, 1951) p. 20f. Reproduced by permission of Penguin Books.

Chaucer's lines on the Prioress, Madame Eglentyne, are the clearest description we have of the manner of eating common in England in the Middle Ages. At the same time we must note that the customs he describes are not in any way specifically English. Habits of eating and drinking had been almost universal in Western Europe for a long time when he wrote in about 1390, and though we cannot say with any certainty either where these customs came from or when they were introduced, it can reasonably be assumed they follow closely on those of the Teutonic tribes. No early writer in England mentions any subject as mundane as that of eating, but the customs Chaucer describes are almost the only answer to the problem in an age when the knife and the spoon were the only implements available.

The later Middle Ages, with which the first part of this book is concerned, present a picture with two aspects. One shows the established custom, which had existed for several hundred years before Chaucer wrote, and of which the central feature is the use of the fingers in eating; the other the early stages of the custom that centres round the use of the fork, which was to displace the medieval usage. As far as Western Europe is concerned it began in Italy, for long the most civilised country there, but its early stages are lost to us in the general lack of early evidence, and we do not meet it before the Italian cookery books of the sixteenth century. The new fashion began in other countries as the knowledge of Italian customs spread. Its beginning in France must be not long after 1533, the date of the arrival in Paris of Catherine de' Medici to marry the future Henri II. In the more distant countries such as England its growth was a slower process, and in England it had to contend with the inveterate English suspicion of all habits introduced from abroad. It had barely begun by the time of the death of Queen Elizabeth I, but by 1660 new features had begun to appear. There was a quite new method of serving meals; the knife acquired a rounded instead of a pointed end, the spoon began to take on the egg-shaped bowl and flat stem of the modern period instead of the fig-shaped bowl and rounded stem of the medieval, and the fork began to come into general use for eating. It seems that the watershed of change from one custom to another was passed in England soon after 1660.

The period between about 1660 and 1900, with which the second half of the book deals, sees the continuation and completion of these changes, as well as an equally radical change in the number, hours, and content of meals. By 1900 four meals instead of three were usual; their hours changed with the ever later hour of dinner. The content was altered by the inclusion of the sweet dishes which appear first in English eighteenth century cookery books. As to the conduct of the meal, the manner of serving and eating food changed greatly. During the later Middle Ages it seems sometimes to have been the cook's purpose to conceal rather than reveal the flavours of the various ingredients in a dish, and meals must have consisted in part at least of *pot pourris*, the flavour more or less disguised by a lavish use of spices. The aim of the modern cook, on the other hand, is to bring out each flavour separately. The manner of service changed also. Instead of placing together on a large platter many of the individual viands composing a course, it became the custom to devote a separate covered container to each of them. Finally, the manner of eating altered with the use of a metal or pottery plate to replace the earlier trencher of bread or wood, and with the habit of using a fork.

The study of the modern period breathes a different air from that of the medieval, the difference between the two being both literal and metaphorical, literal in that during the modern period indoor meals have generally been eaten in a room specially set apart for the purpose, metaphorical in that almost all the early eating customs changed.

There are three things we should bear in mind in dealing with the modern period. The first is a general one. It was during the later Middle Ages and the centuries that followed them that Western Europe coalesced into the national political divisions known today. Relative political stability was accompanied by a measure of economic prosperity, by a gradual increase in population and in the volume of imports of food, and by a rise in the standard of living. The food eaten improved in quality and increased in quantity and variety, and living to eat now became almost as respectable as eating to live. This development reached its climax during the period of French political leadership in the seventeenth and eighteenth centuries. France became the culinary as well as the political leader, and the French terms, *gourmand* and *gourmet*, won general acceptance. *Gourmand*, the earlier word of the two, was originally used for a person who enjoyed eating, and at first there was none of the present suggestion of eating to excess; *gourmet* is a word that originally meant a wine merchant's assistant, but in the nineteenth century rapidly became the more honoured title of the two. We read in A. D. MacQuin's *Tabella Cybaria*, 1820, that

'The *gourmand* unites theory with practice, and may be denominated *Gastronomer*. The *gourmet* is merely theoretical, cares little about practising, and deserves the higher appellation of *Gastrologer*.'

The word 'epicure' has been summoned up from the classical past to signify much the same thing as *gourmet*. The *OED* gives the word three meanings, the first a follower of Epicurus, the second a glutton or sybarite, the third the modern meaning, implying a cultivation of sense and taste. The second and third were both known in the sixteenth century. French influence, however, seems in no way to have been confined to the general adoption of terms such as these. Its most important feature is that French cooking took over the place of primacy occupied in the sixteenth century by Italian. After about 1675 French cooks began to travel over Europe, and this greatly enlarged their reputation. A late example, and perhaps the best known of them, is Antonin Carême, a sometime cook both to George IV and to the Czar Alexander I.

A second point and one with a great influence on meals eaten in the home was the invention of the restaurant, the essential feature of which is the large number and variety of the dishes it offers. The restaurant of today has forerunners, most notable among them being the inn, the chop house, and the Ordinary, but it has no ancestors. It seems to have grown out of the eighteenth century interest in prepared foods for invalids, which occupies a definite place in Mrs. Glasse's *The Art of Cooking Made Plain and Easy*, 1747, and in the shops which dispensed such foods. The word 'restaurant' is not recorded before about 1765. In that year a Parisian named Boulanger opened such a shop and the venture was a success from the start. The scope of the original plan soon widened to include serving ordinary customers on the spot as well as invalids at home; and the restaurant was born.

The third point is the matter of preserving food, a problem of long standing. The Romans were aware of the possibility of using ice in cooling wine, but we do not know whether the indefinite preservation of food was even attempted, and Roman cookery books, such as Apicius *De Re Coquinaria*, tell us nothing. In the Middle Ages the usual method of preserving food was by salt. We know little or nothing of what advances were made in this field during the succeeding centuries. Many experiments were made both in the attempts to preserve food and in allied matters. Some were serious, such as those of Richard Boyle and others; some to our eyes seem merely curious — Francis Bacon is said to have contracted what proved to be his last illness by experimenting in stuffing a chicken with ice. The popularity of ice cream is perhaps another example of the results of these experiments. Of uncertain origin, it was known in Italy in the sixteenth century if not before, and probably came to France with Catherine de' Medici; it seems to have been brought to England in the train of the returning Charles II, and to have been served by him during the 1660's.

The eighteenth century saw a great advance in the adoption of the principle of preservation in a vacuum. There are various claims to have been the introducer; the most convincing story is perhaps that it was a Frenchman, Nicholas Appert (1750-1841). Whoever he was, the first patent for the process is dated at the Patent Office in London in 1810, and the idea seems to have spread quickly across the Atlantic. The use of the tin can was part of the American version of the original; it is said to have been invented by Thomas Kensitt in 1823. The later period saw the rise to the first rank of the idea of preservation at very low temperature, and the refrigerator, run by electricity or gas, is the present answer to the problem.

Part 1

Before 1660

Sources of information

It seems best at the outset to name the sources of information on which these chapters are based. These are of three kinds. First is a large and miscellaneous group of cups and other objects actually used at the table, the earlier ones distinguishable from their modern counterparts in being made for use with little thought of being decorative also. Many show how the practical character that was at first dominant gradually gave way to a decorative one, and how this latter finally eclipsed it, so that towards the end of the period new vessels began to appear, some purely practical, others purely decorative. The vessels that have survived till today are partly decorative, made of gold, silver-gilt or other materials mounted in it, of which the most common are coconuts and nautilus shells, mother-of-pearl, various kinds of pottery, and partly of a plainer type, made of glass, pottery, pewter, leather or wood.

Second is the pictorial evidence. As is generally the case, the English material has to be largely supplemented with parallels from Western Europe. Throughout the period there are manuscript illustrations; they fall by their date into two quite distinct groups. Those earlier than about 1300 are largely Biblical illustrations. They show very little interest in the arrangement of the dinner table and really tell us little about it; they are supplemented by occasional pictures in other media, such as that of the Norman meal before the Battle of Hastings on the Bayeux Tapestry (Plate 1), which are of a similar character. Later manuscripts are of an altogether different type. They show increasing interest in the dinner table, and an ever greater number of details; they are supplemented by pictures which do the same. The miniature of the Duc de Berry at dinner in the *Très Riches Heures* manuscript (Plate 2) is an early French example. The Wedding Feast from the *Life of Sir Henry Unton* painting in the National Portrait Gallery, London (Plate 5), shows the English custom of a rather later date; parallel evidence from other countries is shown in Plates 3 and 4. Apart from these is the long series of pictures of the Last Supper, some of which are merely schematic, while others give many details of how contemporary meals were eaten. Perhaps the most valuable of them is the Ghirlandaio fresco in San Marco in Florence (Plate 6).

Plate 1. The Norman army's dinner before the Battle of Hastings. From the Bayeux Tapestry, Norman-French, 1070-1080. From F. R. Fowke, The Bayeux Tapestry (London, 1873) Plate L

Plate 2. The Duc de Berry at dinner. From the Très Riches Heures manuscript, Burgundian French, 1415. Chantilly, Musée Condé.

Literary evidence is third. In England this begins in the ninth or tenth century with the *Colloquies of Archbishop Aelfric* which, like many medieval books, tells the story in a series of conversations, here between an unnamed person and the officers of the household in turn. In Europe a similar type of book was common, and two examples of the twelfth century on table manners are preserved in German, the first being in dialogue form.* This type is succeeded in the latter part of the period by three others. The first of these are cookery books, of which at least three are preserved belonging to the period just before and just after 1400. The earliest and most famous of them is *The Forme of Cury*, compiled by one or more of the French cooks to Richard II, himself of French birth and upbringing. Two other collections of recipes date from the same period, and there is later supporting evidence.* The first printed English cookery book, *A Proper Newe Booke of Cookerye*, was published about 1575. The second type are the successive Ordinances for the Royal Household, of which the earliest preserved are those issued by Henry VI in 1455. From then until the end of the period every reign is represented except those of Richard III, Edward VI and Mary Tudor; the series continues until the reign of William and Mary, and the last series preserved was issued in 1689.* Finally we must mention a series of books

See G. Schiedlausky, *Essen and Trinken Tafelsitten bis zum Ausgang des Mittelalters* (Nürnberg, Germanisches National Museum, 1956) p. 9.

The Rev. R. Warner, *Antiquitates Culinariae* (London, 1791) p. 1ff.

Many of these appear in *A Collection of Ordinances and Regulations for the Governing of the Royal Household* (London, Society of Antiquaries, 1790). In later notes this book is referred to as *Household Ordinances*.

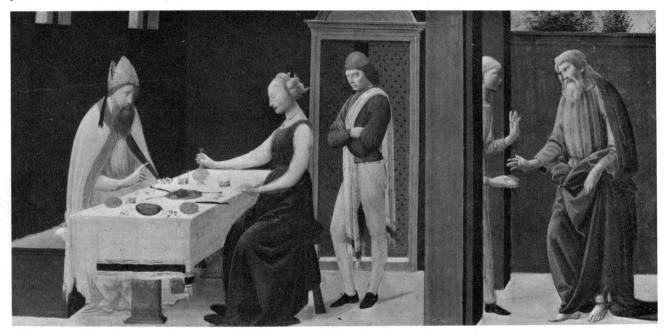

written openly with an educational purpose and for the use of the young, such as the two *Books of Nurture* by Hugh Rhodes and John Russell respectively. These are the relics of a period when education in Western Europe was partly literary, centred round the *Trivium* and *Quadrivium*, and partly practical, to be acquired by serving in a humble capacity in a large household. This aspect of medieval education goes back at least to the twelfth century, when William FitzSteven records that Thomas à Becket, when Chancellor, had a number of boys living in his house to be educated in this way.* There are many of these books of instruction in a number of different languages; the most famous of them, and the most translated, is Erasmus *De Civilitate Morum Puerilium . . . Libellus*, written in the spring of 1530 for Henry of Burgundy, then aged ten and a half. Most of them are content to give instructions which are not very helpful in reconstructing the medieval scene, such as 'keep your knife sharp and clean'—'do not leave your spoon in the dish after the soup is finished'—'take salt on to your trencher with a knife and do not dip the meat in the salt cellar'—'do not shuffle your feet

Plate 3. A Bishop and the Devil at dinner. From a series of paintings of the Miracles of St. Andrew, by Bartolommeo di Giovanni, Italian, Florentine, about 1500. Liverpool, Walker Art Gallery.

See E. J. Furnivall (ed.), *Early English Meals and Manners* (London, 1868) p. vi.

Plate 4. The Feast of the Marriage at Cana, by Hieronymous Bosch (1460-1518). Rotterdam, Boymans Museum.

about or scratch yourself at meals'—'wipe your mouth before you drink'—'and make sure that the cup is kept clean'. Some, such as the two *Books of Nurture* already referred to, are more detailed and far more useful to us. Slightly earlier than these is a French parallel with sections that give incidental information of a generally similar character, the *Livre du Ménagier de Paris*, believed to have been written between 1392 and 1394 by an ageing Paris merchant for the benefit of his young wife, although it is hard to suppose that the whole book is the work of one man.

Most of these books have obviously been written by men, for men or boys to hear, and this is in keeping with the fact that household and kitchen staffs during the later Middle Ages apparently consisted almost exclusively of men. In the list of members of the household of Henry VI,* we may observe that all those mentioned are men, and that women only appear as attendants to Princesses or other exalted persons. In this field, as in others, a change begins to take place late in the period, heralding the much more significant change from the medieval table to the modern. It is one from books written for men to books written for women and about their duties in the house, and reflects the fact that although household staffs still consisted very largely of men during the seventeenth century, there were far more women than before. Early examples show the beginning of two kinds of household book, both of which are especially typical of the modern period. One of them is the book of what, following Mrs. Beeton, we may call 'Household Management', such as Sir Hugh Plat's *Delights for Ladies*, 1609, or Gervase Markham's *The English Housewife*, 1615; the other is the cookery book, quite distinct in type from the much earlier books already mentioned. One of the earliest known examples of this type after *A Proper Newe Booke of Cookerye* of about 1575, is *A Closet for Ladies and Gentlewomen . . . with . . . all kinds of Banqueting Stuffs*, London, 1632.

Setting and furniture

The Chamber—its modern parallel is the sitting room—was the usual setting for dinners eaten by only a small group of people. A miniature of about A.D. 1000 shows 'Luxuria' and two men seated at dinner at a round table.* No background is shown at all, but if any specific setting must be assumed the Chamber is by far the most likely. Much later the treatise *For to Serve a Lord* of about 1500 tells how, after dinner, presumably eaten in the Hall, the guests retire to the Chamber to rest; after resting they consume a light dessert. The place of eating this is not given, but may be assumed to be the Chamber. The custom of dividing dinner between two different settings still exists in colleges at the older universities, and among the Benchers of the Inns of Court.

The Hall was the place for meals attended by a larger number, and is shown used in this way in a great many illustrations, of which Plate 4, a Flemish painting, is the clearest reproduced here. In the sixteenth century it came to be supplemented by the separately built Banqueting House. This was an independent building, sometimes of painted canvas on a wooden framework and sometimes of brick, several storeys high and with wine cellars beneath, as, for instance, in Henry VIII's hunting lodge of Nonsuch.* The most common sixteenth century meaning of the word 'banquet' is given by the *QED* as either 'a slight repast between meals

Cotton MS. C.VIII, Folio 15 in the British Museum, illustrated by John Hampson, in *The English at Table*, London, 1944, p.11.

Plate 7. Winter, from a set of engravings of The Four Seasons, *by Abraham Bosse (1602-1676). New York, Metropolitan Museum of Art, Dick Fund.*

Plate 8. The Vyvyan Salt, silver-gilt and enamel. Ht. 15¾". English, London, 1592-3. London, Victoria and Albert Museum. Crown Copyright Reserved.

John Dent, *The Quest for Nonsuch* (London, 1962) p. 125f.

sometimes called a running banquet' or 'a course of sweetmeats, fruit and wine served either as a separate entertainment or as a continuation of the principal meal, but in the latter case, in a different room; a dessert', and the Banqueting House was a place for eating this dessert course, as we should perhaps call it now, rather than for consuming a Banquet in the modern sense, and for looking at entertainments of various kinds. When Capulet, in Shakespeare's *Romeo and Juliet* I. v, trying to prevent his guests leaving the house, says that a 'trifling, foolish Banquet' is being prepared, we may be certain that he is using the word in the old, not the modern, sense.

The Banqueting House, often a much less permanent building than the house proper, is perhaps a suitable bridge from meals eaten indoors to those eaten out-of-doors. Very occasionally Great Feasts eaten out-of-doors are recorded in written descriptions and illustrations, though always in a warmer climate than that of medieval England is known to have been; one such is a feast given by Archbishop Baldwin in Trier in 1308.* It seems likely that records of feasts such as this were kept precisely because they were rare occurrences, and that the illustration in this particular case was added partly to show that many of the servants were mounted on horseback.

It is too much to say that there is no record anywhere of meals having been eaten out-of-doors, but the history of the period gives us very little reason to suppose that the modern picnic has any medieval forerunners in England.*

When we turn from the setting of meals to the furniture used for them in the Hall, we find that little is recorded. Inventories of furniture in medieval English Halls are extremely sparse in number of pieces and details, and we can observe, if dimly, only two that are likely to have been permanent. The first is the Dresser, the English equivalent of the French *Dressoir* and the German *Tresur** and the ancestor of the later Court Cupboard.

This was a piece of furniture about five to six feet in height and three to four feet wide. There were three shelves, of which the top normally served as the Cup Board, for the display of pieces of gold and silver of value, and John Russell's *Book of Nurture* instructs the learner to 'Set your Cup Board with gay silver and silver-gilt . . .'* Whether the bottom or third shelf served any purpose we do not know, since it was just above the floor level; in the few manuscript illustrations which show this piece it is always empty. Immediately below the top shelf there was a cupboard in the modern sense of the word, the bottom of it forming part of the second shelf. This piece appears in a number of manuscript illustrations of the fifteenth and sixteenth centuries,* where its resemblance both to French and to later English cupboards is very strong.

That this was the normal household Cup Board is made clear by these illustrations, as is the fact that it could be placed in any one of the private rooms. That it was the only type is in contradiction to the manuscripts, both English and German, which lay down rules for the Cup Board. It is agreed by these that a Duke of high rank may have a Cup Board with five shelves, a Duke of lower rank four, a nobleman below a Duke three, a Knight Banneret two, and an ordinary gentleman one shelf only. Such a cupboard is referred to in George Cavendish's sixteenth century *Life of Cardinal Wolsey:*

'There was a Cup Board made, for the Chamber, in length, of the breadth of the nether end of the same Chamber, six desks [sc. shelves] high, full of gold plate, very sumptuous, and of the newest fashions; and upon the nethermost desk garnished all with gold, most curiously wrought . . . This Cup Board was barred in round about that no man might come nigh it . . .'*

Similar words are used in Holinshed's *Chronicle* describing a feast given by Henry VIII; reference is made to 'a cupboard of twelve shelves all filled with plate of gold, and no gilt plate'. These suggest what must have been a large and very cumbrous piece of furniture, and we cannot be surprised

Schiedlausky, *op. cit.*, fig. 5.

G. Grigson, *Country Life*, August 20, 1959, p.54f.

For the *Dressoir*, see Schiedlausky, *op. cit.*, fig. 20. For the *Tresur*, see Plate 22 *ibid*.

Furnivall, *op. cit.*, pp. 131-2, lines 231-2.

T. Wright, *History of Domestic Manners* (London, 1862) p. 379, etc.

George Cavendish, *Life of Cardinal Wolsey* (London, 1887 ed.) pp. 101-2.

Plate 9. *Salt, silver-gilt and mother-of-pearl. Ht. 7¾″. English, late 16th century. Toronto, Lee of Fareham Collection.*

that no examples exist today. How common such Cup Boards were, and how exactly the rules were observed that governed the number of shelves each rank might have, we cannot say.

The second of the more or less permanent pieces of furniture was one serving the purpose of a side or serving table, which seems to date as far back as the sixteenth century.* Some examples survive and perhaps descending from them are the late sixteenth and seventeenth century three-shelf buffets, of which there are a few in existence.* They seem to have been made for the service of meals, wherever eaten.

See Schiedlausky, *op. cit.*, p. 35.

One is illustrated in *The Connoisseur Period Guide, Tudor Period* (London, 1956) Plate 17.

The original dining table was not a permanent piece of furniture. Its top consisted of boards laid on trestles, thus giving ultimate rise to the modern expressions 'bed and board' and 'boarding house'. Household inventories frequently mention tables with several of these trestles. This kind of non-permanent table continued in use for a long time, and was gradually superseded either by a permanent table consisting of the boards and the trestles nailed together, or by tables with corner legs. Both these types seem to have come into use in the later fifteenth century. The practice of ornamenting the legs with large 'pineapple' or 'cup and cover' bulges did not come into fashion until the second half of the sixteenth century, and a simpler kind was in use by the middle of the seventeenth.

The normal seat in the medieval Hall was the bench, either with or without a back. We may suppose that the members of the early Court of King's Bench actually sat on a bench of just the same kind that was used in the Hall. There must have been many without backs, though none are known today; that they were both usable and used for other purposes is borne

Plate 10. Triangular trencher salt, silver-gilt. Length of sides 3⅝". English, 1607-8, maker's mark G in a shield. Toronto, Lee of Fareham Collection.

out by Sir Thomas Malory's description of the attack on Sir Lancelot by Sir Agravain, Sir Colgrevance and others: 'and meanwhile they had gotten a great forme from the Hall and therewithal they rashed at the door'.* The back of the bench, when there was one, consisted of three horizontal pieces of wood nailed to the uprights, and such a bench is a fairly common feature of household scenes of the fifteenth century and later.* It was a mark of honour to have a separate seat at the dinner table, generally a stool (Plate 4); when Shakespeare's Macbeth speaks of dead men 'pushing us from our stools' (III. iv) it must, in view of the circumstances, have been to stools used in the dining hall that he was referring. Chairs were known to the Romans* and the use of the term *ex cathedra* 'from the chair', must be of early origin,

Malory, *Morte d'Arthur* (London, 1927 reprint) Book XX, Chapter IV, p. 439.

Wright, *History of Domestic Manners* (London, 1862) p. 427. A scene from a 15th century Valerius Maximus manuscript in the British Museum is published in Eileen Power (ed.) *The Goodman of Paris* (London, 1928) Plate 16.

G. M. A. Richter, *Ancient Furniture* (Oxford, 1926) figs. 303-5, 307; Joan Liversidge, *Furniture in Roman Britain* (London, 1955) Plates 27, 28, 32, 35.

Frank Davis, *A Picture History of Furniture* (London, 1958) fig. 5.

Description de L'Isle des Hermaphrodites, said to be by Thomas Cortus; Cologne, 1724 edition, p. 97.

but the first chair of a modern type dates from the twelfth century and is a feature of the famous carving from Chartres, now in the Louvre, showing St. Matthew writing his Gospel.* There is a French reference to chairs (*fauteuils*) at the dinner table in the *Description de L'Isle des Hermaphrodites*, a satirical work purporting to be a description of life at the court of Henri III.* In later medieval England the chair used for any purpose was always rare, and must have been normally reserved for the Master of the household. It was slow to become popular in England and in some of the earlier Inventories is missing altogether; a change took place at the end of the period and is seen in an engraving of the Dutch artist Bosse, which shows a row of chairs, and a page laying a dinner table (Plate 7).

Meals of the day

Our information about the meals of the day is restricted to Royal and other great Households, and it is only about them that we have enough information to write a chapter such as this. So far as such households are concerned, there were two formal meals a day during the Middle Ages, dinner and supper, and a lighter and informal one which developed into the modern breakfast was also eaten. Dinner was in the middle of the day,

usually between 11 and 12 o'clock. The orders for the Household of the 'Princess Cecill' (Cicely Neville, Duchess of York), the mother of Edward IV, who reigned from 1461-83, explain that the preparation of dinner began at 11, when a special meal for the Carvers and officers employed during the main dinner took place. The time of the main dinner in the Princess's household is not stated, but we may perhaps assume that it was 12 o'clock. The hour for supper was 6, and Chapter 45 in the Eltham Ordinances,* made in 1526, order that 'When the King and Queen are not present dinner is to be served at 11 o'clock before noon, or near thereupon, and supper at 6'.

As to breakfast, the allowance of food to each member of the Household is given in the *Liber Niger* of Edward IV* as food 'for his Chamber and breakfast', and the word 'breakfast' is twice used in the almost contemporary Accounts of Sir John Howard.* It consisted at first of bread, beer or ale, and wine, and we may draw the conclusion that breakfast began literally as a matter of breaking the fast of the night by a very light meal. The Account Book of Henry Algernon Percy, fifth Earl of Northumberland, dating from 1512, shows that the idea of breakfast as a larger and more varied meal was already gaining currency; reference is made to the consumption of beef, mutton, salt fish, herring and sprats.* The next stage is shown in the 1610 Establishment of Prince Henry's Household, which gives a description of

Household Ordinances, p. 151.

Ibid., p. 25.

Manners and Household Expenses in England in the 13th and 15th Centuries (London; Roxburghe Club, 1841), pp. 340, 503.

Reprinted in Warner, *Antiquitates Culinariae*, p. xlix f.

the Prince's breakfast, mentioning 'manchet, cheate fine and cheate ordinary [all three being varieties of rolls], beer and wine, one service of beef and one of mutton and two chickens'.*

Household Ordinances, p. 317.

At dinner and supper those present sat in the order of precedence given in Chapter 4. This very detailed list is paralleled by the lists of the food served to the various ranks as given in the Royal Ordinances. It seems from these that the King and Queen were served with the richest and most varied food, and that the richness and variety gradually diminished as the list proceeded: it was not desirable that one of a lower rank should eat the food prepared for one of a higher. Three sets of Ordinances* deal with food.

Ibid., pp. 100f, 174f, 317f.

Those for the Household of George Duke of Clarence in 1469 list the types of food ordered, but say nothing about who was to eat it, while the Eltham Ordinances of 1526 for King Henry VIII and the Orders for the Household of Prince Henry in 1610 give complete lists, together with the rank of what may have been the presiding person at the table. These lists are of such a character as to make us ponder seriously on the exact point at which the later Middle Ages drew the line between normal eating on one side and what St. Thomas Aquinas called the Deadly Sin of Gluttony on the other. The Clarence Ordinance does not deal directly with the diets of individuals in the household, but considers the matter of food from the point of view of the purchases made in bulk. These are listed in full; the list begins with wheat, wine, sweet wine, beer and ale, and then goes on to meat (mutton, beef, veal and pork) and fish (ling, salt fish, stock-fish [dried fish] salmon, sprats, herrings red and white, eels, sturgeon), oil, honey, acates (Provisions purchased*) and such things as wax, candles, spices with other ingredients, and cloth. In view of the fact that the list is dated 1469, several years before Vasco da Gama rounded the Cape of Good Hope in search of lands rich in spices, the list of ingredients is very informative. It includes pepper, saffron, ginger, cloves, mace, cinnamon, nutmeg, greynys (?), saunders, turnsoyle (both these were terms for colouring matter for food), as well as dates, jardens (Jordon almonds) and valaunces (Valencia oranges), prunes and anise, liquorice, sugar (two entries), cassyns (?), green ginger, charle-

This is the *OED* definition; the word was soon used much more generally to mean unspecified 'Necessaries for Diet'.

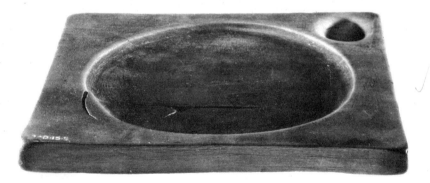

Plate 13. *Trencher, sycamore.* 7¾″ x 7″. *English, probably about 1600. Toronto, Royal Ontario Museum.*

quinces (a pulp of quinces), comfits, currants, figs and raisins (four sorts), and rice.* Part of this list is repeated by the Clown in Shakespeare's *A Winter's Tale*, IV. ii, as purchases to be made for the sheep-shearing festival.

Household Ordinances, p. 103.

The Eltham Ordinances, the second set of the group dealing with food, were issued by Henry VIII from the palace at Eltham in 1526; the section that concerns us is headed 'A declaration of the particular Ordinances of Fares for the diets to be served to the King's Household, the Queen's Grace and the Sides [sic] with the Household . . .' Before we go on to deal with these we must note one feature about these lists. Diets for the King and Queen are listed under the heading 'Flesh Day' and 'Fish Day', but diets for the other ranks are listed under headings for Sunday, for Tuesday or Thursday, and for Monday or Wednesday, followed by entries for Friday dinner and Saturday supper. Whether no meals were served during the

Plate 14. Pepper pot, silver-gilt. Ht. 4³⁄₁₆″. English, London, 1581-2, maker's mark I.H. Toronto, Lee of Fareham Collection.

thirty or so hours between these last two is never stated, but it must be assumed that something was eaten. That this regulation for meals is connected with the rules of fasting seems certain, but we know nothing of its exact application; towards the end of the Middle Ages it seems that the 'Flesh Day' and 'Fish Day' rule was relaxed, and this is reflected in the latest of these sets of Ordinances.

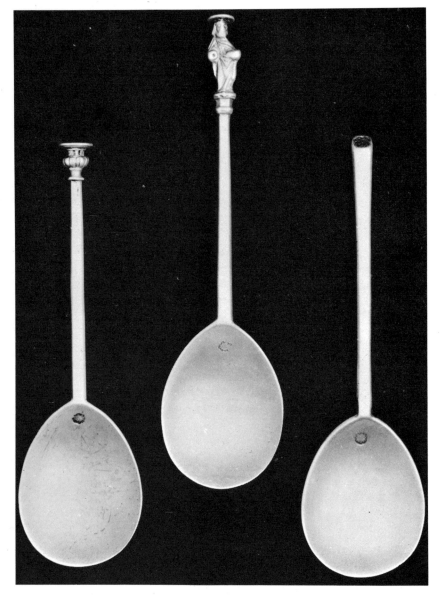

Plate 15. Spoons, silver. (1) Apostle (London, 1570-71). Length 7″. (2) Seal-top. Length 6¼″. (3) "Slip i' th' Stock". Length 6½″. (2) and (3) unmarked, English, 16th-17th century. Toronto, Royal Ontario Museum.

The Eltham Ordinances give a detailed list of what food was eaten by what rank. It would take too much space to reproduce the list in full, and the richest diet is given here as an example.

The Diett For The King's Majesty And The Queen's Grace, Of Like Fare, In All Two Messes, As Followeth.
On a FLESH DAY.
Dynner.

Cheat Bread and Manchett,	16
Beare and Ale,	6 gal'
Wyne,	1 sext

Flesh for Pottage,
Chines of Beef, 2
Rammuners in stew or cap', 1 mess
Venison in bewz' or mult', 1
Pestells of Reed Deere, 1
Mutton, 2
Carpes or Yong Veale in
Arm' farced, 1
Swanne, gr'Goose, Storke
or Capons of Gr', 2
Conyes of Gr', 1
Fryanders, baked Carpe, 1
Custard garnished or 1
Fritters 1

Supper.

Cheat Bread and Manchett, 16
Beere and Ale, 6 gal'
Wyne, 1 sext
Flesh for Pottage,
Chickens in crituary, Larkes,
Sparrows or Lambe stewed,
with Chynes of Mutton, 1
Giggots of Mutton or
Venison, stopped with Cloves, 1
Capons of gr' 2
Conyes of gr' 1 mess
Phesant, Herne, Shovelard, 1
Cocks, Plovers or Gulles, 1
Swete dowcetts or Orange, 1
Quinces or Pippins, 1

Second Course

Jelly, Ipocras, Creame
of Almonds, 1 mess
Pheasant, Herne,
Bitterne, Shovelard, 1
Partridges, Quailes or
Mewz' 1
Cocks, Plovers or Gulles 1
Kydd, Lambe or Pigeons, 1
Larkes or Rabbetts, 1
Snyters, Pulletts or
Chickens, 1
Venison in fine past, 1
Tarts, 1

Blank-mange or other dish, 1 mess
Kydd, Lambe or Pejons, 1
Partridge or Quailes, 1
Godwitts Brewez', 1
or Teales, Pulletts,
Chic'pip', 1
Rabbetts or Larks, 1
Tarte, 1
Fruite, 1
Butter and Eggs,
Venison or other Baked
Meates, 1
Fritter, 1

Fruit with powder or
   piscards,   1
Butter and Egges

On a FISH DAY.

Dynner.

Cheat Bread and Manchett,	16
Ale and Beare,	6 gal'
Wyne,	1 sextar'
Herring,	1 mess
Pottage,	1
Organe Lyng,	1
Poudred Eales or Lamprons	1
Pyke,	1
Playce or Gurnard,	1
Sea Breame or Soalles,	1
Congers, Door,	1
Porpose, Seale,	1
Carpe, Troute,	1
Crabbs, Lobsters,	1
Custard,	1
Rascalls or Flage,	1
Claver Salmon,	1
Whyting,	
Haddocks, Mulletts,	
or Base,	1
Tarte Closed,	1
Frytter,	
Fruite,	1

Second Course

Second Pottage,	1
Sturgion pr'vel r'	1
Byrt or other dish,	1
Breame or other dish,	1
Tench,	1
Perch, or other dish,	1
Eles with Lampreys rost,	1
Chynes of Salmon broyled,	1
Crevez,	1
Shrympes,	1
Tarte,	1
Frytter,	1
Fruite,	1
Baked Pepins, Oranges,	
Butter and Eggs	

Light is thrown on the source of fresh water fish in the fifteenth century by an entry in the Howard Accounts.* Sir John Howard writes that in the second year of Edward IV he had stocked many of the ponds on his estate, and that the fish he had put there were roach, tench, perch, bream great and small, and carp great and small. He goes on to say that five years later the ponds had been damaged and that the fish had disappeared. He has therefore restocked them with the same fish as before.

The Establishment of Prince Henry's Household in 1610, the last ordinance dealing in detail with food, gives another list, of which the first section is headed 'For the Prince His Highness'.

Manners and Household Expenses, p. 560f.

For The Prince His Highness Breakefast.

Manchet,	2
Cheate fine,	2
Cheate,	4
Beere,	3 gallons
Wine,	1 pitcher
Beefe,	1 service
Mutton,	1 service
Chickennes,	2

Upon A FLESH DAY.
Dinner.

Manchets, fine,	5
Cheate, fine,	4
Cheate, course,	12
Beere and ale,	10 gallons
Wine,	3 pitchers
Mutton boyled,	2 services
Veale boyled,	2 services
Chickennes boyled,	3
Pigeons boyled,	4
Beefe,	1 service
Veale,	2 services
Shoulder of Mutton,	1
Legge of Mutton,	1
Goose,	1
Capon,	1
Chickens,	5
Parteridges,	2
Conyes,	3
Lambe,	quarter
Lapwings,	3
Conyes to bake,	1 pye
Peares,	1 pye
Chewets,	1 service
Custard,	1
Tart,	1

Supper.

Manchet, fine,	5
Cheate, fine,	4
Cheate, course,	12
Beere and Ale,	10 gallons
Wine,	3 pitchers
Mutton boyled,	1 service
Veale boyled,	1 service
Chickens boyled,	3
Pigeons boyled,	4
Mutton rost,	2 services
Veale rost,	2 services
Legge of Mutton,	1
Tongues,	2
Capon,	1
Chickens,	5
Lapwings,	3
Parteridges,	2
Larkes,	18
Conyes,	3
Lambe,	quarter
Conyes to bake,	1 pye

Tongues,	2
Peares,	
Dulcets	1 service
Tart,	1

For Collation After Supper.

Manchet,	1
Beere,	2 gallons
Wine,	1 pitcher

Upon a FISH DAY.
Dinner

Bread, beere, Ale and Wine,
  as upon a flesh day.

Chickens boyled,	4
Mutton boyled,	2 services
Veale boyled,	1 service
Lambe boyled,	quarter
Shoulder of Mutton, rost,	1
Veale rost,	2 services
Legge of Mutton,	1
Capon in greace,	1
Chickens,	5
Partridges,	2
Lapwings,	3
Larkes,	18
Conyes,	3
Peares,	1 pye
Custard,	1
Tart,	1
Lyng,	1 service
Pyke,	1 service
Carpe,	1
Whiteings,	1 service

Supper

Breade, Beere, Ale and Wine
  as at dinner aforesaid

Chickens boyled,	4
Mutton boyled,	1 service
Veale boyled,	1 service
Lambe,	quarter
Mutton rost,	2 services
Veale rost,	2 services
Capon,	1
Chickens,	5
Partridges,	2
Snypes,	5
Conyes,	3
Lapwing,	3
Peares,	1 pye
Dulcetts,	1 service
Tart,	1
Lyng,	1 service
Pyke,	1
Carpe,	1
Whiteings,	1 service
Haddocks,	1 service

Plate 16. *Carving knife and fork, and set of nine knives with ivory handles, with one of nine matching forks. Length of carving knife* 10¼″; *of other knives* 8⅞″. *The blade of each knife is ornamented with an engraving of one of the Saints. German,* 1637. *Toronto, Royal Ontario Museum.*

Here we turn aside momentarily to note that in the earliest records the number of wines drunk appears to have been small. In a letter of about A.D. 1200 Giraldus Cambrensis refers only to Claret, 'New Wine', and Mulberry wine,* while later in this century the Leicester Accounts* refer to red wine, white wine, Gascony and Bastard. The Howard Accounts of nearly two hundred years later* mention red wine and Gascony as before, Malmsey, Claret and Spanish wine. The contemporary Clarence list names Malvesie, Romenay, Osey (sweet French wine), Bastard Muscadelle under the heading of Sweet Wines, but gives no details under the plain title Wine. Prince Henry's list in 1610 mentions Gascony wine and Sac. (Plate 26).

Although vegetable growing in France begins in the time of Henri IV (1589-1610) under the guidance of Olivier de Serres, there seems to have been a long gap in time before there were similar developments in England. Not until the second half of the eighteenth century does English vegetable growing really begin on a large scale. We cannot avoid the conclusion that medieval meals in most households must largely have consisted of fresh or salted meat and fish, with such few vegetables and fruits as were in season.

One of the most necessary features of the medieval dinner table, mentioned regularly in the Royal Household Ordinances, was salt. The Salinator is one of the early household officers to appear in the *Colloquies of Archbishop Aelfric*, written probably in the tenth century, and addresses his interlocutor with the words 'What man enjoys fresh food without the flavour of salt? Who refills his cellars or containers without my art? All the butter and the cheese would perish without me to look after them.'* Salt is described in the Ordinances as being of two types, Bay Salt and White Salt. Bay Salt was that used for preserving food, and in the absence of all methods of refrigeration a great deal must have been used for this purpose. Salt must have been specially necessary for use in preservation at the slaughter of animals which took place every autumn. It is in keeping with this that one of the early London Companies to be incorporated was that of the Salters, which dates from 1307. No distinction whatever of quality seems to have been made between fresh and salted meat or fish, either in the *Colloquies of Archbishop Aelfric* or at any time during the Middle Ages, and in the rare texts where they are mentioned together they appear side by side as equals. Thus in a graffito on the walls of the Guildhall of the Holy Cross at Stratford-upon-Avon, of a date about 1450, there appears a notation of a fish dinner provided for the burgesses of the town, which reads in part 'item, in piscibus salsis vii d . . . item, in piscibus recentibus' (sum not given).* White Salt, on the other hand, was that used regularly at the table, and was put into the Great Salt and the other containers.

Pepper is in a different case. It is first known to have been imported into Alexandria and so to the Mediterranean during the Roman Empire, from southern India. The import on a large scale does not seem to have survived the decline of the Empire in the West, and when we hear of pepper in early medieval sources, as we very occasionally do, it is of something regarded as extremely precious. It does, however, seem that there was some trade throughout most if not all of this period, and our next information of its use in England is of a guild of Pepperers, mentioned in a London Pipe Roll of 1180. These Pepperers were one of several groups which in 1428 went to form one basis for the Worshipful Company of Grocers (probably those who sold *en gros*, wholesale and not retail) incorporated in London in that year. It was not until some time after 1500 that pepper and spices began to be common in Europe and the earliest surviving English pepper pot belongs to the year 1563.

Mustard is a plant of which different species grow in many countries, England being one. In some form it was known to the ancients, and is referred to both by Greek and Latin authors and in the New Testament. The history of mustard during the earlier part of the Middle Ages is obscure,

Plate 17. Spike (a forerunner of the fork), silver, English, ? 9th century. London, British Museum. Crown Copyright Reserved.

H. A. Monckton, *A History of English Ale and Beer*, London, 1966, p. 40; the passage is referred to at greater length here.

Manners and Household Expenses, p. 1f.

Ibid., pp. 153, 380, 501.

'Quis hominum dulcibus perfruitur cibis sine sapore salis? Quis repplet cellaria sua sive promptuaria sine arte mea? Ecce Butirum omne et caseum perit vobis, nisi ego custos adsum . . .' T. Wright, (ed.), *A Volume of Vocabularies* (London, 1882), p. 9.

R. L. Hine, *Relics of an Uncommon Attorney* (London, 1951), p. 209.

Plate 18. Poison cup, silver-gilt with rock crystal lining. Ht. 9¾". German, Augsburg, about 1580, by Ulrich Schonmacher. Toronto, Lee of Fareham Collection.

and we do not meet it in English records before the Leicester Accounts for 1289. In the Accounts of Sir John Howard* both mustard and mustard seed are mentioned, and in Shakespeare's *A Midsummer Night's Dream* one of Titania's attendants is called Mustard Seed. Contemporary with this is the recipe in Sir Hugh Plat's *Delights for Ladies*, 1609.

Manners and Household Expenses, pp. 229, 399, 528.

Mustard Meale

'It is usuall in Venice to sell the meale of Mustarde in their market, as we doe flower and meale in England: this meale by the addition of vinegar in two or three daies becometh exceeding good mustard, but it would bee much stronger and finer, if the huskes or huls were first divided by searce or boulter, which may easily be done, if you drie your seedes against the fire before you grinde them. The Dutch iron handmils, or an ordinarie pepper mil may serve for this purpose. I thought it verie necessarie to publish this manner of making your sauce, because our mustard which we buy from the chandlers at this day is many times made up with vile and filthy vinegar, such as our stomack would abhorre if we should see it before the mixing thereof with the seeds.'

This, with its reference to 'Sauce', does not seem to bear out the common modern belief that the sets of three casters of late seventeenth and early eighteenth century English silver were for salt, pepper and mustard, while the much larger single caster was for sugar. The subject is treated more fully below.

Of the medieval history of sugar we know very little. Something began to be heard about it in England soon after 1200, and before 1230 a group of Jews from the Maghreb district of what is now Morocco brought sugar canes to Sicily; it is perhaps significant that the earliest English text on the subject, dated 1299, refers among other types to 'Zuker Marrokes'. Nothing seems to have come of this, and we must suppose that the usual sweetening element in food continued to be honey, as in the days of Apicius. The Spaniards in the sixteenth century re-imported sugar canes into Europe, first from Madeira and later from Spanish America, and it was then that sugar began to gain real popularity; we may suppose that one reason for the slowness of the growth in popular esteem is that sugar, like tea in the next century, was at first believed to be chiefly medicinal in its qualities. The period of sugar's real popularity is dealt with in the next section.

Before we leave the subject of the Royal Ordinances we must note that the one point on which none of the Ordinances dealing with food is explicit is the precise meaning of the word 'dish'. We know what the large dishes in use were like from the wooden example in Plate 4 and the pewter one in Plate 28, while on the other hand many of the fifteenth and sixteenth century authors speak of 'a dish of meat' or 'ten dishes of meat'; but it is not entirely clear what the word meant. Was it merely a large dish platter? Was it the amount of meat such a platter would hold, and if so could this be of more than one kind? The question is carried to an extreme point by an Ordinance made by James I in 1604, 'First, Whereas Our-selfe and Our deare Wife the Queen's Majestie, have bene every day served with 30 Dishes of Meate; nowe, hereafter, according to this Booke signed, Our Will is to be served but with 24 Dishes every Meale, unless when any of Us sit abroad in State, then to be served with 30 Dishes, or as many more as We shall command.'*

Household Ordinances, p. 299.

It is quite impossible to believe that James I intended 30 of the large platter-dishes to be on his table. None of the dinner tables in Plates 2–7 or the later ones in Plates 31–32 would have had enough space for them, and we must also wonder whether enough meat would have been available to fill them. We cannot but conclude that the word 'dish' really meant a measure of quantity, probably of more than one kind of meat.

To list the food served at any given period during the Middle Ages is sometimes comparatively simple. To say how any of it was cooked and brought to the table is difficult or impossible. In the surviving English books

Plate 19. *The Cup-bearer. From* The Feast of Ahasuerus and Esther, *by Henning von der Heide* (*fl.* 1487-1520). *German, about* 1496. *Lübeck, St. Anne Museum.*

of medieval recipes mentioned above, such as *The Forme of Cury*, there are lists of recipes interspersed with occasional notes to the cook, for instance, 'Nota. Cranes and herons shall be armed with lardes of swine and eaten with ginger' or this, 'Nota. Peacock and partridges shall be parboiled and roasted, and eaten with ginger', and many of the contemporary books repeat these. The recipes are, however, difficult for the modern reader for two reasons especially. One is that the language is often difficult to understand; the other is that, like all books of recipes up to and including some of those published during the nineteenth century, these books are extremely vague when it comes to giving exact amounts and weights. A fair example is the recipe which follows: the wording is unchanged, but the spelling has been modernized.

Plate 21. *Drinking horn, silver-gilt mounts. Ht.* 10¾″. *English, about* 1450. *Toronto, Lee of Fareham Collection.*

Hares in Paddel [a saucepan]

'Take hares and slea [skin] them and pick them clean, and hew them in gobbets, and put them in a pot with the blood, and seethe them, and when they be [done] enough, take them up and do them in cold water, and cleanse the broth into a fair pot and do other good broth thereto; and take almonds and bray them, and temper it with the same broth, and put it thereto, and onions parboiled and minced and do it in the pot and set it on the fire, and let it boil, and do thereto powder of cloves and of canell, and maces, and a little vinegar; then take the flesh well washed, and the bones clean picked out, and do them in the pot of the broth, and let it boil, and serve it forth.'

No details of quantities are given, and this recipe would be very difficult

Plate 20. *Harold at Bosham. From the Bayeux Tapestry, Norman French,* 1070-80. *From F. R. Fowke,* The Bayeux Tapestry (*London,* 1873) *Plates III and IV.*

to follow. These books, in fact, are chiefly valuable to us because they include several sample menus for both a Fish Day and a Flesh Day. These are repeated from one to another book, and the first of each runs as follows (the spelling again is modernized).

Service on a Fish Day

'At the first course, oysters in grave [gravy?], and baked herrings, and pike, and stock-fish, and merlings [whitings] fried. At the second course, eels in grave, and porpose, and galantine; and therewith conger, and salmon fresh, and dory roasted or gurnard sothen [seethed or softened], and baked eels and tart. At the third course, rose to potage [?], and cream of almonds; and therewith sturgeon, and whelks, and great eels, and lampreys roast, and tench in jelly; and therewith daryoles [a pasty of meat, herbs and spices], and leche-fryes, make to frit and friture[?].'

Service on a Flesh Day

'Boar's head enarmed, and bruce to potage [?]; and therewith beef, and mutton, and pestels of pork; and therewith swan and coney roasted, and tart. At the second course drope [?], and rose to potage, and therewith maudelard [mallard?] and pheasant, and chickens sersed and roasted, and malachis baded [?]. At the third course coneys in grave, and boar in brase [?] to potage; and therewith teels roasted, and partridges, and flampoyntes [pie or tart decorated with points of pastry].'

Apart from these sample menus there is little information at all easy to put to practical use. There are full recipes for some of the dishes, listed in very summary form and with no details, as being prepared for the Royal Household. There are also recipes for soup, many if not all being for the thick variety, or potage; for fish, giving a number of the fifteenth century equivalents of some of the less easily understood descriptive terms seen on restaurant menus today; and for meat and game. The latter perhaps reach their highest point in a recipe headed 'at a Feast Royal Peacocks shall be dight on this manner', and continuing:

'Take and slee off the skin with the feathers, tail and the neck, and the head thereon, take the skin with all the feathers, and lay it on a table broad, and straw thereon ground cummin; then take the peacock and roast him and baste him with raw yokes of eggs; and when he is roasted take him off, and let him cool awhile, and take and sew him in his skin and gild his comb and so serve him forth with the last course.'*

Warner, *Antiquitates Culinariae*, p. 63.

Conduct of meals

When the tables and benches or stools had been placed in position the next step in preparation for a meal was the laying of the table cloth. It does not seem at all likely that the cloth was laid directly on the table, for towards the end of the Middle Ages the table came to be permanently covered by a Table Carpet. These carpets are referred to in literary sources and there are two examples of embroidered table carpets in the Victoria and Albert Museum. Table carpets also appear in Dutch *genre* paintings of the seventeenth and eighteenth centuries, and are still in use in Holland today. It seems probable that the cloth was laid over the table carpet, rather than that the latter was removed when the former was used: in Holland the carpet is left underneath the table cloth. How far back in time the use of table cloths goes is not certain; the earliest surviving references are Roman* and the first example which has any claim to be called medieval is a mid-sixth century mosaic of the Three Angels visiting Abraham on the walls of San Vitale in Ravenna, begun in A.D. 546. From that point onward medieval illustrations both of this scene and of the Last Supper always show a table cloth, and so do secular dinner scenes when they begin to appear.

Some of the earlier sources are quoted in W. A. Becker, *Gallus* (London, 1898) p. 476.

Most of the books of instruction mention the table cloth, and two at least describe the method of laying it. In the later Middle Ages three cloths seem to have been often used in England, the bottom one being laid evenly over both long sides as the modern cloth is, and each of the two upper ones laid so that it fell down near the ground on one long side of the table and covered the top but did not come over the edge on the other: the ends of the table are not mentioned. This at least seems to be the most satisfactory interpretation of what Wynkyn de Worde in the *Boke of Kervynge** and John Russell in his *Book of Nurture** mean by their descriptions.

Furnivall, *op. cit.*, p. 268.
Ibid., p. 129, line 185.

'And whan ye laye the clothe, wype the borde clene with a cloute [cloth], than laye a clothe, a couche, it is called, take your felawe that one ende, & holde you that other ende, than drawe the clothe straught, the bought [?] on the utter [outer] edge take the utter parte, & hange it even than take the thyrde clothe, and lay the bought on the inner edge and laye estat [each?] with the upper parte halfe a fote brode.'

This is Wynkyn de Worde's version: his 'cloute' is the lower cloth, the 'clothe' and 'thyrd clothe' being the two upper cloths of our description. A ceremony of the laying of the cloth is described in the Articles ordained by Henry VII for his Household in 1494.* The main table was covered first, and after it the officer in charge (usually the Panter or Server) proceeded to lay cloths on the Cup Board and the side tables.

Household Ordinances, p. 119.

The use of three cloths instead of one was a late development, perhaps intended to impede what must have been a common feature of the medieval dinner table, the presence of a number of domestic animals about the diners' feet. This explains the *Boke of Curtasye's* instruction 'do not stroke the dog or cat during the meal.'* Dogs were strictly forbidden in the Royal Bakehouse in the *Liber Niger* of Edward IV* and in the Eltham Ordinances they are absolutely forbidden in the Court as a whole, 'except for some few small spaniels for Ladies or others'.* A dog appears in the foreground of the Marriage at Cana painting in Plate 4.

Furnivall, *op. cit.*, p. 302, line 107.
Household Ordinances, p. 70.

Household Ordinances, p. 150.

The books of instruction direct that after the table cloth was laid the first thing to be put on it was the principal Salt. Even today there are many superstitions about salt, evident especially in the habit of throwing a pinch of it over the left shoulder when any is spilt, and during the Middle Ages they were much stronger. The sources agree that the Salt should be put on the table first, and those that carry the story through to the end of the meal agree further that it should be taken off last. We know little of the principal Salt as it was used in England before about 1500; the fourteenth century is said to have seen the introduction of Salts in many curious forms, especially animal; monkeys, elephants, lions are all mentioned in the literature. By the

Plate 24. Wine cup, silver-gilt. Ht. 8¼". English, London, 1617-18, maker's mark T.I. Toronto, Lee of Fareham Collection.

Furnivall, *op. cit.*, p. 23. This explains the well for salt in the wooden trencher illustrated in Plate 13.

F. M. Stenton (ed.), *The Bayeux Tapestry* (London, 1957) Plate 49.

C. C. Oman, *Medieval Silver Nefs* (London, Victoria and Albert Museum, 1963) *passim*.

Roman sources are collected in W. A. Becker, *op. cit.*, p. 477.

T. Wright (ed.), *A Volume of Vocabularies* (London, 1882), p. 132.

end of the fifteenth an hour-glass shape was usual, later varied to include cylinders and other vertical shapes (Plate 8). The decorative character was very strong, and the usual material in those that survive is silver-gilt; a mother-of-pearl example of the late sixteenth century is shown in Plate 9. Other types of salt cellar must have supplemented the large showy one, and are referred to or implied by a number of the books of instruction, but we know nothing of their details. 'Likewise, do not touch the salt in the salt cellar with any meat; but lay salt honestly on your trencher, for that is courtesy' says *The Babees Book*.* Small salt cellars of silver or silver-gilt, round or triangular, are preserved from sixteenth century France and Germany, and from England rather later. An example dated 1607 is shown in Plate 10.

Nothing was placed on the medieval dinner table without a practical purpose; the Salt stands out in being decorative as well. It shares this character with the Nef, its French and German counterpart. The Nef originally came into favour during the early Middle Ages, and what may be a Nef appears on the Bayeux Tapestry.* It was originally a drinking vessel, but very soon became what nowadays might be called a Status Symbol (Plate 2), and came to be made in ship form. (Plate 11). The practical purpose, where it still existed was generally served by a small salt cellar in the rigging. The Nef was never common in England and never made there and so is outside the scope of this book.*

The practical purpose of the salt gradually gave way to that of the trencher salt, which from about 1550 comes to supplement and finally to replace wholly the earlier type. At the same time the decorative purpose was transferred to various table ornaments which lacked a practical side altogether. There were many of these. One of the most striking was produced by the interest in mechanical toys common to many countries at this time, though it seems likely that most of them were made in Germany. A German example by Matthäus Wallbaum, bearing the mark of Augsburg and to be dated about 1585, is shown in Plate 12. The figure is that of Diana on the Stag, one of the most popular subjects. It moves along the table by a clockwork mechanism concealed in the base.

Pepper, as has been noted, was quite widely known in England during the Middle Ages, especially after the incorporation of the London Grocers Company. What may be the earliest English pepper pot, an oriental rock crystal bottle mounted in silver-gilt is in the Victoria and Albert Museum. The pepper pot in Plate 14 is of silver-gilt, and bears the hallmark of London, 1581-2 and the maker's mark I.H. Pepper must have been quite common at this time to justify a caster containing as much as this does.

Containers which date from this period, made for other flavouring ingredients, are much less common. Upright casters for sugar, either with curved sides or straight sides in a 'lighthouse' shape, begin to survive about the middle of the seventeenth century. Mustard has been mentioned above, and is believed to have been taken dry at this time, though Sir Hugh Plat speaks of it as having been eaten in liquid form. No containers, however, survive until the eighteenth century.

The early rule was that as soon as the Salt was on the table other objects could be placed there, first and foremost napkins, loaves of bread to be cut into trenchers, and spoons. The napkin was in use in antiquity* but is said to have gone out of fashion during the prolonged insecurity which marked the end of the Roman Empire in the West, and not to have returned until the fifteenth century. Although medieval illustrations give no suggestion that napkins were in use, the fifteenth century seems very late, and a 'hemmed napkin' is mentioned in the *Dictionary* of John de Garlande* in the early thirteenth. Most of the late medieval written sources mention napkins, and 'two nappekynes' worth 20 pence are mentioned in an Inventory in the *Lincoln Chapter Account Book* of 1420; few of the writers give any details of size or use. The general rule for several centuries was that when not in use the napkin should be placed over the left shoulder or the left arm: ' . . . put one towel around your neck, one side of which have on your left arm.'* It is in this way that napkins appear in Plates 3 and 5, but in the fifteenth and sixteenth centuries, as elaborate lace Falling Collars came into use, there was a fashion for wearing the napkins around the neck to protect the collar. We do not know whether this custom was usual in England in the seventeenth century, but how general the use of napkins was, is shown by one of Pepys's complaints about the Lord Mayor of London's banquet mentioned in the *Diary* on October 29, 1663, that 'we had no napkins.'

With the napkin a loaf of bread, in the early years at least, was placed before each guest. This was 'trencher bread', and the guest was expected to cut pieces from the loaf to make a trencher or flat platter for his own use. Many sources from the fourteenth century onwards agree that the Master's personal bread for eating was to be new, other bread on the table a day old, household bread three days old, and trencher bread four days old.* The *Ménagier* adds that it should be 'half a foot wide and four inches high, baked four days before and let it be brown . . .'* Other sources tell us that the trencher was to be cut in two thicknesses of bread, of which the upper one was to be divided vertically in four and the lower in three.* The treatise *For to Serve a Lord* of about 1500 is the first to mention wooden trenchers, 'trenchers of tree', as well as those of bread;* and we are allowed to assume that wooden trenchers were gradually replacing the earlier ones of bread. A wooden trencher, perhaps of about 1600, is illustrated in Plate 13, and a number of parallels to it are known.* We cannot be surprised that wood replaced bread as the material, since wooden trenchers must have been more practical. Pepys says in the *Diary* for January 10, 1660-61 'Thence to Tom Pepys and bought a dozen of trenchers and so home', and we must assume that these were wooden ones. That the wooden trencher was the ancestor of the modern plate is indicated by the fact that about 1600 the phrases 'plate trencher' or 'trencher plate' were in use.* The word 'plate' was slow in replacing the word 'trencher' and when Ralph Verney writes a letter to his wife in 1647 about a presentation he uses 'trencher plates', when by modern standards it would have been the word 'plates' only.

'If he absolutely refuses money (as I hope he will not) then you must lay it out in some such plate as you think fittest; I think six trencher plates and a pair of little candlesticks (without sockets) of ten pounds, would do well. . .'*

Pepys attended the Lord Mayor of London's banquet in October 1663. He sat at the Merchant Strangers' table, and one of his complaints was that there was 'no change of trenchers, and (that they used) wooden dishes'. It is perhaps a mark of how rapidly customs were changing that Pepys should make this complaint. The 'change of trenchers' he refers to is mentioned by a number of the written sources, and seems to have taken place whenever there was need for it. That 'trencher plate' was a common term is further shown by an entry in the Tart Hall Inventory made in December 1641: 'In a Cubbard in the Greate Room five shelves, on the uppermost six dozen and eight of white earthen trencher plates'.*

Of the three implements we use nowadays for eating, spoons during the Middle Ages seem usually to have been provided by the host, and are referred to in a great many of the written sources. At the same time they do not appear in any of the early medieval illustrations, which are several hundred years older, and we cannot be certain that this is not due to the fact that the practice then was for everyone to carry his own spoon; spoons are absent from almost all the earlier Inventories. Some of the earliest examples are, as we might expect, of wood, and have large oval-shaped bowls and very short handles, perhaps because they were meant to be carried. These, however, are German.* Silver ones were moderately common, and examples of ivory, rock crystal and mother-of-pearl are all known. It is probably the result of the accidents of preservation that all the

John Russell's *Book of Nurture* (Furnivall, *op. cit.*, p. 129, line 193).

Furnivall, *op. cit.*, p. 120.

Eileen Power (ed.) *The Goodman of Paris* (London, 1928) p. 239.

Furnivall, *op. cit.*, p. 300.

Ibid., p. 367.

Victoria and Albert Museum 7028-1891; cp. Owen Evan Thomas, *Domestic Utensils of Wood* (London, 1932) Plate.

Peter Erondell in M. St. Clare Byrne, *The Elizabethan Home* (London, 1940) p. 65.

Lady Charlotte Verney (ed.) *Memoirs of the Verney Family during the Civil War*, vol. II, p. 279, letter of Ralph Verney to his wife, October 10, 1647.

Lionel Cust, 'Notes on the Collections formed by Thomas Howard, Earl of Arundel and Surrey, K. G.' *Burlington Magazine*, vol. 20, 1911-12, p. 99.

Schiedlausky, *op. cit.*, figs. 9, 36.

remaining medieval English examples of a similar period are of either silver (Plate 15) or latten (an alloy containing copper). They have oval or fig-shaped bowls, and round handles much longer than those of the German examples, with knops at the ends.*

Knives were generally carried by the guests, and Claudius Hollyband in his French grammar makes the schoolmaster,* presiding over dinner, say 'Every man draw his knife', and at the end of the meal, 'Every man clean his knife and replace it in his sheath.' The view that the guest owned the knife may be corroborated by the fact that none of the early books of instruction visualises their provision by the host, and in view of this silence we cannot really be sure whether the table knife was used for eating or merely to help in cutting up the meat; a change at the end of the period is perhaps shown by a set of ten knives with pointed blades and ivory handles (Plate 16), made in Germany and dated 1637. Knives seem from the remaining examples to have been commonly pointed during this early period, and this suggests that they were used to carry the food to the mouth, a practice which many of the books of instruction warn against, for instance the *Boke of Curtasye*: 'Do not put your knife to your mouth . . .'* Knives of this period are seen in Plate 4. It is suggested that they began to be ornamented on the blades when they came to be made in sets and laid out on the table.

Ibid., p. 12.

M. St. Clare Byrne, *The Elizabethan Home*, p. 10.

Furnivall, *op. cit.*, p. 302.

Plate 25. Soup bowl, earthenware. Diameter 9″. English, 14th or 15th century. Toronto, Royal Ontario Museum.

It seems that the original purpose of the fork was to hold the meat still while it was being carved, and therefore that forks for carving antedate those for eating at the table. Whether other implements for this purpose preceded them we do not know. The Carver in Plate 2 must be assumed to be holding the joint with his left hand while carving it with his right; implements such as single spikes may also have been used (Plate 17). That medieval forks were used for various purposes is shown by a will of 1463, bequeathing 'my silver fork for green gyngour'.* Forks for eating at the table were early in use, at least by the fourteenth century in the more civilized centres, such as Byzantium, and were known in France and Germany by the later fifteenth or sixteenth century. They probably began to be known in England at about the same time. That forks were perfectly well known in England then is shown by the casual nature of the reference in the *Itinerary* of Fynes Moryson. Speaking of the Italians, he says:

'At the Table, they touch no meate with the hand, but with forke of silver or other mettall, each man being served with his forke and spoone, and glasse to drinke.'*

Bury St. Edmunds Wills (Camden Society) 40.

Fynes Moryson, *An Itinerary*, (Glasgow, 1908), vol. IV, p. 98.

and Peter Erondell, writing towards the end of the reign of Elizabeth I, speaks of 'little silver forks to go beside each plate'.* Thomas Coryate in his *Crudities*, 1611,* claims to have been the introducer, but it is clear that they were beginning to be generally known in England at the time.

M. St. Clare Byrne, *op. cit.*, p. 65.
Wright, *History of Domestic Manners* (London, 1862) p. 457.

In its form, the medieval fork bears the same relation to its modern counterparts as do the spoon and the knife. Early examples have two steel tines, straight, much longer than they were later, and with each tine in round section tapering to a sharp point. The forks shown in Plate 16 are examples. Only towards the mid-seventeenth century does the number of tines increase, and the modern style begin to appear.

The pair of implements, at first knives and forks made with matching handles, appears in France and Germany in the sixteenth, in England in the seventeenth century. The knife in these early pairs is large and generally pointed, the fork much smaller. The pairing of spoon and fork belongs to a much later period.

One more point about the table needs to be mentioned. Towards the end of the Middle Ages, when the sternly practical character of the early table arrangements had begun to pass away, there grew up the habit of adding to the dinner table new and partly decorative features of a quite different

Plate 26a. Wine holder, earthenware, about 1300. Ht. 11⅝". Toronto, Royal Ontario Museum.

character, known as Sotelities (the word is very variously spelt). We first hear of these in one of the late fourteenth century English cookery books, in a Menu for a Flesh Day:

'At the second course was a soteltee Seint-Jorge on horsebak and sleynge the dragun. At the third course was a soteltee, a castel that the Kyng and the Qwhene comen in for to see how Seint-Jorge slogh.'*

Household Ordinances, p. 450.

It is a matter of some uncertainty what the Sotelitie was made of. The ingredients may have varied between one time and place and another, but considering the variety of the figures as well as the great popularity of almonds at the medieval dinner table, it does seem likely that the Sotelitie was often made of marzipan. This certainly seems to be the case with the examples mentioned in George Cavendish's *Life of Cardinal Wolsey*:

'Anon came up the second course, with so many dishes, subtelties, and curious devices, which were above a hundred in number, of so goodly proportion and costly, that I suppose the Frenchmen never saw the like. The wonder was no less than it was worthy indeed. There were castles with images in the same; Paul's church and steeple, in proportion for the quantity as well counterfeited as the painter should have painted it upon a cloth or wall. There were beasts, birds, fowls of diverse kinds, and personages, most lively made and counterfeit in dishes; some fighting, as it were, with swords, some with guns and crossbows, some vaulting and leaping; some dancing

Plate 26b. Wine holder, 16th century. Ht. 6 3/16". Drinking Cup, 16-17th century. Ht. 3 7/8". Both earthenware. Toronto, Royal Ontario Museum.

with ladies, some in complete harness, jousting with spears, and with many more devices than I am able with my wit to describe. Among all, one I noted: there was a chess-board subtilely made of spiced plate, with men to the same; and for the good proportion, because that Frenchmen be very expert in that play, my lord gave the same to a gentleman of France, commanding that a case should be made for the same in all haste, to preserve it from perishing in the conveyance thereof into his country.'*

George Cavendish, *op. cit.*, p. 103.

F. M. Stenton (ed.) *The Bayeux Tapestry* (London, 1957) Plate 49 and Colour Plate IX.

F. D. MacKinnon, *Inner Temple Papers* (London, 1948) pp. 12-15.

We do not know what means were used to summon the party to the table for meals, or indeed whether there was any recognized method of doing so. A figure in the Bayeux Tapestry uses a hunting horn (Plate 1),* but this is a member of Duke William's army on campaign, and it may or may not have been a common practice. In the 1930's the Inner and Middle Temples re-enacting an ancient practice, summoned their members to dinner with a horn, sounded half an hour before the meal.* At one time and place in Germany a trumpet was used for this purpose, but none of the English sources refer to this, and again we cannot say whether it was a practice followed anywhere in England.

The English sources begin in the Hall itself, and this fact seems to imply that there was no special summons. 'The guests being led in by the host wash their hands . . . then they sit down,' says Comenius in *Janua Linguarum*, 1632.* With these words we are at once plunged into an uncertainty, whether it was before or after the public washing of hands that grace was said. Comenius implies that it was after hands had been washed, and is followed by other sources in this opinion, but *For to Serve a Lord* says that as

Wright, *History of Domestic Manners* (London, 1862) p. 459.

soon as the guests had assembled in the Hall grace was said, and only after it was the hand washing carried out at a side table, with ewer, basin and towel, after which the guests sat down.* It is difficult for us today to believe that grace preceded the washing of hands, but our modern conditions are too different for assumptions of this kind to be relevant.

Furnivall, *op. cit.*, pp. 368-9.

The washing of hands before the meal was normally done at a side table, but it seems that sometimes the jug and basin were brought to the diner. 'When you see your Lord go to meat be ready to fetch him clear water and hold the towel until he has done . . .' says *The Babees Book*.* This was certainly the common practice, but a slight addition to it seems to have been made in the sixteenth century, and is mentioned by George Cavendish 'with that the water was brought them to wash before dinner, to which my Lord called my Lord of Norfolk to wash with him, but he refused of courtesy . . .'* The jug and basin used for this purpose appear in a fourteenth century French manuscript,* and are referred to in *The Book of Nurture*: 'set . . . your ewery board with basins and ewers, and hot and cold water, each to temper the other.'* Soap was known, but was not in general use, and the more or less public ceremony must have been intended, perhaps hopefully, to demonstrate to the diners that all hands were clean before the meal started. The material of which the jug and basin were made must normally have been either pottery or metal, probably brass, though late in the period there was a change, and silver basins and ewers of the sixteenth century are known. Because of its use, this ewer was sometimes referred to either as a *manilium* or an *aquamanilium*. Theophilus, *De Diversus Artibus* III, 75, refers to but does not name this vessel; the probably rather later *Chronicle* of Christian of Mainz speaks of 'urcei . . . quos manilia vocant . . .' During the fourteenth century there seems to have been a fashion for the use of fanciful shapes for these as for other water holders, but later examples are simpler.

Furnivall, *op. cit.*, p. 5.

George Cavendish, *op. cit.*, p. 164.

Wright, *History of Domestic Manners* (London, 1862) p. 156, fig. 109.

Furnivall, *op. cit.*, pp. 131-2.

If grace had not been said already it was said by the Almoner after the guests had sat down, and he immediately placed an Alms Dish on the table before the Master.* The Almoner seems to have had a number of very varied duties of this kind; in the undated Additions to the Eltham Ordinances we read 'The Almoner shall give diligent attendance within the house daily, gathering all the broken meats throughout the said house and to distribute the same to the poor people, without embezzling any part of the same . . .'* The Alms Dish remained on the table throughout the meal. The Carver placed two loaves of bread in it immediately, perhaps to ensure that God was served before man, and there were other ceremonies connected with it; the *Boke of Curtasye*, for instance, directs that whenever a piece of meat is cut up or a fish divided for the guests a small piece must be placed in the Alms Dish. The Leicester Accounts tell us something about the part that the Poor played in the life of the great household, and the importance of the Alms Dish at meals is one example to which there are many parallels.

Furnivall, *op. cit.*, p. 323.

Household Ordinances, p. 239.

If the rank of the Master or of any one of the guests was far above that of the others, he was placed at a table by himself, and served separately. Such an arrangement, with Lady Macbeth sitting alone is implied in the banquet scene in Shakespeare's *Macbeth*, III. iv. Otherwise most medieval illustrations show guests sitting on one side only of a long table with the Master usually in the centre, the other side being used for service; the Echternach Codex of 1040 is the first to show this tradition, and is followed by many others.* It does seem from the written sources that these illustrations simplify the matter, and that in the later years at least the guests were divided according to rank at a number of much smaller tables. This must explain the rather enigmatic opening of *Macbeth*, III. iv. Here Macbeth, addressing his guests, says 'You know your own degrees, sit down.' The Wedding Feast in the Unton painting (Plate 5) shows the guests sitting on both sides of the table. Early in the period the rule seems to have been that the highest ranks dined first, and we may assume that by the time the

Schiedlausky, *op. cit.*, Plate 1.

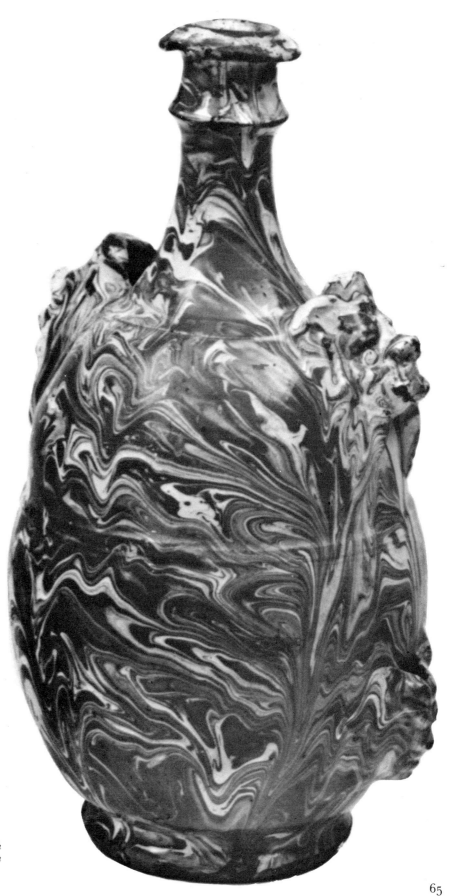

Plate 26c. Wine holder, marbled ware, late 17th century. Ht. 10¾″ (possibly French, but found in England). Toronto, Royal Ontario Museum.

lowest were dining the highest were ready for supper; but later in the period everyone ate at the same time, sitting in a strict order of precedence. Schiedlausky remarks that the placing of the guests at table was a matter of great importance, and that it is made clear in the Arthurian Romances that it was because of this that the Round Table was invented.* A number of the books of instruction refer to this matter of precedence, and how guests of one rank must not in any way be confused with those of another. Attitudes such as this are indicated by the *Ménagier's* passage 'At the bidding of Monseigneur the President, the Procureur de Roi was seated above the Avocat du Roi',* and the point is put even more clearly in John Russell's *Book of Nurture*. 'Each estate or rank shall sit in Hall at a table by itself and not meet those of another rank.'* The matter of precedence, so far as it refers to the food served to different ranks, has been dealt with already. Here we must consider its other aspect. Two of the books give a complete list of the degrees of precedence, beginning with the Pope, who 'has no equal', and ending with a Gentleman and Gentlewoman. John Russell's *Book of Nurture* gives the ranks as

Group 1: The Pope, the Emperor, the King, Cardinals, Princes, Archbishops, Royal Dukes

Group 2: A Bishop, a Marquis and an Earl are co-equal
Group 3: A Viscount, a Legate, a Baron, a Suffragan or a Mitred Abbot, three Chief Justices, the Lord Mayor of London
Group 4: A Cathedral Prior and a Knight Bachelor, a Dean, an Archdeacon, a Knight, an Esquire of the Body, the Master of the Rolls, a Puisne Judge, a Clerk of the Crown, the Mayor of 'Callais', a Provincial or a Doctor of Divinity, a Prothonotary, the Pope's Legate or Collector

67

Group 5: A Doctor of both Laws, an ex-Mayor of London, a Sergeant at Law, a Master of Chancery, a Preacher, a Master of Arts, other Religious Orders, Parsons and Vicars, Parish Priests, City Bailiffs, a Sergeant at Arms, Merchants, a Gentleman, a Gentlewoman.*

This list is the same as that given in Wynkyn de Worde's *Boke of Kervynge*,* and is so very detailed that we cannot but wonder how often and how seriously these rules were in the event observed. The order of precedence is in many ways different from the modern one, but perhaps the most surprising feature is the fact that the only woman mentioned is the 'Gentlewoman', who comes at the very end. This, in fact, is one of the instances in which the pictorial and the literary evidence are in conflict. The latter, here at least, seems to exclude women, though we cannot be certain that the wife of any given person who is listed is not intended to be included with the husband. The former, on the other hand, shows women present at dinner not only on occasions such as weddings, but at many other meals as well.

Dinner began with a procession of servants bearing the food from the kitchen. 'Friar John, at the head of the Stewards, Sewers, Yeomen of the Pantry and of the Mouth,* Tasters, Carvers, Cupbearers and Cupboard Keepers, brought . . .' says Rabelais in *Pantagruel*,* describing a procession

of this kind, of which the leader seems often to have been the Carver. This procession is further referred to by Hugh Rhodes in the *Book of Nurture*. 'The manner of serving a knight, squire or gentleman: in some places the Carver doth use to shew and sit down and goeth before the course and beareth no dysh, and in some places he beareth the first dysh, and maketh obeysaunce to his Master and setteth it down before the degree of a knight . . .'*

Before the meal the Server had orders to cover over the dishes as soon

Furnivall, op. cit., p. 185.

For this phrase cp., e.g., Queen Elizabeth's Household Book, Household Ordinances, p. 296.

Rabelais, Works, ed. by Urquhart and Motteux (London, n.d.) p. 368.

Plate 28. Platter, pewter. Diameter 20". English, probably 17th century. Toronto, Royal Ontario Museum.

Plate 29a. Black jack, leather. Ht. 12⅜", English. 16th-17th century. Toronto, Royal Ontario Museum.

Furnivall, op. cit., p. 67.

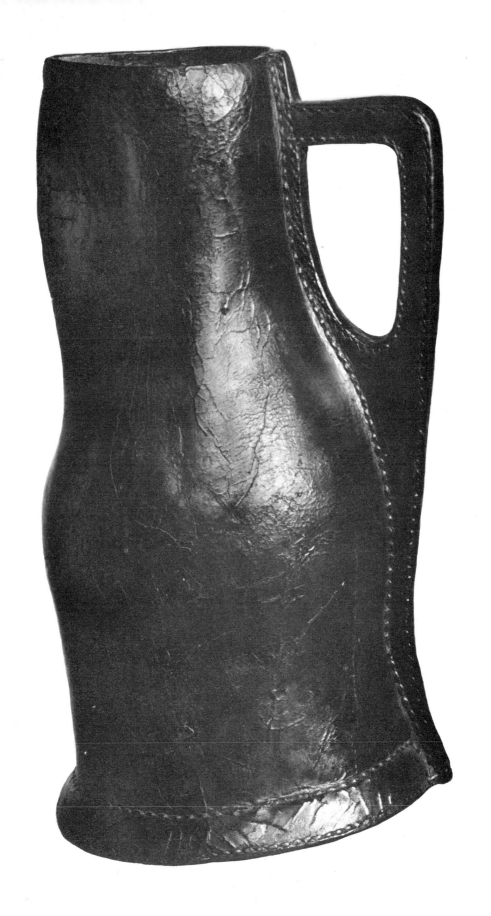

as the cooked meat was placed in them, the covers to remain there until he himself lifted them off at the High Table; the *Ménagier* notes that it was a particular honour to be served with covered dishes. The reason for this is not stated, but may be assumed to be connected with the fear of poison.* This was one of the perennial fears of the later Middle Ages, against which elaborate precautions were taken, though the reputation of the Borgia family suggests that these were not always very effective. One of them was a public test carried out by the Server and either the Carver, the Chamberlain or, according to the *Boke of Curtasye*, the Cook,* as soon as the food was placed on the High Table.* The Test consisted of their eating a piece of the food to be served and drinking part of a bowl of soup; it is shown in progress in a miniature in a 'Conquêtes de Charlemagne'* manuscript written in late fifteenth century France. This public test for poison is seldom mentioned in English sources, and we must assume that the reason for this is that most of the sources were written for people who would not be required to carry out the test themselves without further instruction. A late stage of this test, although the writer clearly did not understand the character or purpose of what took place, is described by Thomas Platter as taking place at Nonsuch: 'When they [sc. the attendants] had handed over the food a gentleman removed the cover, while the lady-in-waiting served and carved a large piece off, which she gave to the guard who had carried it in, and was supposed to eat the portion, though they generally took it out or merely tasted a morsel. Two of them brought wine and beer which was also poured out and tasted . . .'

Platter and his party visited the Lodge when Queen Elizabeth I was in residence. *Travels in England*, 1599, mentions how the test was carried out in the dining hall even when the Queen dined alone in her private apartments.* It is inexplicable that none of the Royal Ordinances of any date, despite their very detailed description of the Household, makes any mention at all of this test. For those who did not order it two means of partial protection were available. Poison in food could be partially guarded against by keeping the knife, the spoon and, when it came into use, the fork and also the salt under lock and key. This was done in what seems to have been an elaborate box known as a *Cadenas*, described in later medieval French sources and probably introduced into England from there; it is referred to at the Coronation of Charles II in 1660. English examples of the Caddinet (the Anglicized French term), belonging to the latter part of the seventeenth century, are considered later, in Part 2. Poison in drink could be similarly guarded against by vessels lined with materials believed to change colour in some way when they touched anything containing poison. Of these materials the most important were narwhal horn, rhinoceros horn, rock crystal, agate or serpentine. It was a common habit in several countries to have a tankard with a complete inner lining made of some such material. A German 'poison cup' with a lining of rock crystal is shown in Plate 18.

The test for poison being concluded, the Carver dominated the scene for some time. To be a Carver was one of the honourable positions of the later Middle Ages, but we have to notice that there are two stages to be clearly distinguished. Until about 1400, as *The Forme of Cury* and its contemporaries suggest, soft foods to be eaten mainly with the spoon seem to have been common. This perhaps helps to explain how it happens that the spoon is the earliest eating implement preserved, though meat must have been eaten to some extent to justify the appointment of a Carver in the first place. A change seems to have occurred about 1400. The miniature of the Duc de Berry is French evidence, Plate 2, and the Ordinances that deal with food are English evidence, for the view that in the fifteenth century the eating of meat in joints became more common, and it is perhaps in line with this that carving and table knives are both preserved from the fifteenth century onwards.

The first effect of this change on the position of the Carver seems to have

Eileen Power (ed.), *The Goodman of Paris* (London, 1928), p. 237.

Furnivall, *op. cit.*, p. 323.
Ibid., p. 196.

Schiedlausky, *op. cit.*, fig. 20.

Thomas Platter, *Travels in England*, 1599, edited by Clare Williams, (London, 1937) pp. 194-5; John Dent, *The Quest for Nonsuch* (London, 1962), p. 178.

been the appointment of assistants to him, recorded in the fifteenth century Ordinances, but towards the end of the sixteenth the position seems to disappear altogether. Ben Jonson's evidence, given in full in Part 2 below, is that by about 1610, when the play containing it was written, a special Carver was no longer always appointed, and the task of Carving had begun to pass into other hands; succeeding centuries saw a continuation of this process.

In the fifteenth century there were many semi-technical terms belonging to the Carver's office, many of which are given by Wynkyn de Worde; the Household Ordinances of Henry VI mention two 'Kervers', both of them Knights and each attended by one Squire and two Yeomen, who formed part of the Household and ranked directly after the members of the nobility and before all the other household officers.* The Clarence Ordinance of 1469 enlarges the list slightly by mentioning a Carver, a Cup Bearer and a Server, who ranked after the Duchess and her attendants, the Chamberlain and the Almoner;* each was attended by one person. The *Liber Niger* of Edward IV refers to the Carvers and Cup Bearers as being Bannerets or Bachelor Knights, and adds 'In the Noble Edward's days [sc. Edward III], worshipful Esquires had this service, but now thus for the more worthy . . .',* and again, 'Oftentimes these [Esquires of the Body] stand instead of Carvers and Cup Bearers . . .'* In other households the Carver was sometimes the Lord's Squire. Chaucer refers to this in *The Squire's Tale*,

> 'Now the Lord's Squire was standing by and heard
> The tale as he was carving, word for word.'*

Household Ordinances, p. 16.

Ibid., p. 100.

Ibid., p. 32.

Ibid., p. 36.

Chaucer, *Canterbury Tales*, ed. Coghill (London, 1951), p. 342.

Plate 30. Cup, birch. Ht. 8⅛″. English, 16th to 17th century. Toronto, Royal Ontario Museum.

John Russell's *Book of Nurture* (Furnivall, *op. cit.*, p. 137, line 317).

Schiedlausky, *op. cit.*, figs. 7, 18, 19. cp. Victoria and Albert Museum, Cat. Nos. 22239-1855; M602-1910; 1165-1864.

M. St. Clare Byrne, *op. cit.*, p. 10.

Manners and Household Expenses, pp. 192, 257.

A figure who might be the Duc de Berry's Squire is shown in the act of carving in Plate 2. Towards the end of the period carving became almost a fine art; schools were set up in Italy, books written on the subject, and the art practised on wooden models.* When the Carver might have to deal with anything from a small bird to the proverbial 'ox roasted whole', we can well believe that this practice was advisable. The Carver was provided with special knives, often in an elaborate leather case. Several sets of these, mostly German, are in existence, and date from the later fifteenth and sixteenth centuries. The most complete of them contained two large carving knives, a fork and a knife-sharpening steel, together with other implements. Many have small knives, occasionally a small fork, and rather more frequently what seems to be a needle, perhaps for use in preparing a slain animal for cooking.*

The Carver must have aimed at filling the large dishes of wood or pewter brought to him from the individual tables by the many servants shown, for instance, in the 'Conquêtes de Charlemagne' miniature. The guests, as we have said above, sat in groups according to rank, and appear to have had each his own trencher before him, while the food was brought to the table on the dish, each person then helped himself with the bare hand. It seems too that a soup bowl of the type of that shown in Plate 25 was placed between every two guests and that each of them had his own spoon, which must account for the insistence of many of the books of instruction on taking your spoon out of the bowl when you have finished.

The earliest illustrations always show the diners bare-headed, as they would be now, but at a rather later date it seems to have been usual to keep the hat on during meals. This habit lasted well into the seventeenth century. During the reign of Elizabeth I Hollyband explains this by saying 'None of you putteth off his cappe at supper, lest some heare might fall in the dishes',* and Pepys, writing many years later, says in 1664 that he 'caught a strange cold in my head by flinging off my hat at dinner'. The practice of keeping the hat on is seen in some of the figures in the Wedding Feast in the Unton painting, though not in that of Sir Henry Unton himself; it is also seen in all the adult figures in the engraving reproduced on Plate 32. It seems at latest to have died rapidly after the Restoration, and now survives only in a few isolated places.

The manner of eating with the hands is described by a small number of authors, most notably Chaucer in the lines quoted at the outset. Perhaps the most revealing light is thrown on it by the third line, 'Nor dipped her fingers in the sauce too deep'. The existence of numerous sauces is to be assumed from the immense lists of food given above, and several are described in the two *Books of Nurture*. We do not, however, know anything about the containers that they were served in, and none remain now. Comenius, writing during the seventeenth century, says 'sawce is laid out [sc. on the table] . . . in sawcers', and a low-sided open dish would seem to suit this description best, but we cannot tell with certainty what it was like. The Howard Accounts, in the mid-fifteenth century, refer twice to 'sawsers' but no details of them are given.* One occasion is that of one of the periodical refittings of Sir John Howard's ship, when a large number of 'sawsers' was ordered from the turner's in Ipswich, and we may assume from this that they were made of wood; this, however, was for use on shipboard, and the use of wood may not have been general.

Chaucer's words about the Prioress are a very complete description of how meals were eaten, and help to explain why Ben Jonson, just over two centuries later, said in *The Devil is an Ass* that forks had been introduced from Italy 'to the saving of napkins'. The fact that carving was probably done in a rather wholesale manner, and that the individual ate with his fingers and had a knife and spoon but no fork to help him divide the meat into small pieces, must explain the constant warnings of the books of instruction against the habit of picking the teeth with the knife. This is a theme which recurs in nearly all these books, and the fact that the blades of knives were pointed at this time, as they appear in Plates 3 and 4 as well as in many other illustrations and in actual examples, seems to confirm that the knife could be used for picking the teeth as well as for eating. Proper tooth picks were prized possessions, and were frequently of aromatic rather than plain wood, myrtle and rosemary being among the favourites.

The meal was accompanied by music and dancing of various kinds. An illumination of the thirteenth century shows a single horn player seated on the floor close to the dining table, part of the marriage feast of David and Michol.* A rather later, though similar scene, with a number of standing musicians is shown in a British Museum manuscript of the fourteenth century.* Later representations of the musicians show them in two ways. In one, they are standing on the floor of the Hall, sometimes, through pictorial necessity, shown playing almost into the ears of the diners; an engraving by Michael Wolgemut* is a German example of this, and a late picture in a German stained glass window dated 1633 is another.* In the second type, the musicians are gathered in a 'musicians' gallery' above the heads of the diners, and this is clearly shown in Plate 19 and perhaps in Plate 4. To have music accompanying the meal was a practice that lasted for a long time. It is referred to in Pepys, 'I expected musique, but there was nothing but trumpets and drums, which displeased me',* and, often in a different form, is followed today. As an alternative to music there were other possibilities: a Biblical manuscript of the fourteenth century shows Salome standing on her hands before Herod.* Another variant was the Masque, shown in progress in Plate 5. Yet another, this time German, was a procession of servants dressed as mummers, who are seen in an illustration in *Der Weiss Kunig,* a book describing the exploits of Maximilian I of Hapsburg.*

Many of the materials discussed already are best illustrated in drinking vessels, and mention of these brings up the question of the Cup Bearer. The Cup Bearer's position, like the Carver's, was one of great honour. In the early seventeenth century it is mentioned in Ordinances and Regulations before and not after the Carver. The Establishment of Prince Henry's Household of 1610 refers to 'the Gentleman Cup Bearer, Carver and Server', and the Household of Henrietta Maria, Queen of Charles I, included two Cup Bearers, three Carvers, and two Servers, each with one attendant.* A Cup Bearer is seen in Plate 19.

Drinking vessels were placed on the table only for small parties. On the more formal occasions, drinking vessels were placed on the Cup Board and under the care of the Cup Bearer. A diner who wished to drink called for a cup of wine, which was specially filled and brought to him by the Cup Bearer. After drinking, he handed the cup back for rinsing and replacing on the Board. Italian glass vessels serving the same purpose are shown in Plates 3 and 6.

Of the drinking vessels, the first to be mentioned is the Horn. Ox horns are referred to in Caesar's *Gallic War,** as having been used by the Gauls and Germans; they or their mounts have been found in the Baltic area and northern Germany,* and later examples at Sutton Hoo.* Gold horns dating from this period were found at Gallehus in Schleswig. They are possibly late Roman in date, though not Roman in origin.* A later use of horns is mentioned in a twelfth century English Bestiary: 'There are fierce bulls of the wild ox in Germany, which have such immense horns that, at the royal tables, which have a notable capacity for booze, the people make the receptacles for drink out of them.'* Imitations of the form in glass* and in pottery* have also been found. Ox horns were in use during the Middle Ages for various purposes; Athelstan gave the church at Durham 'three horns made from gold and silver',* which must have been for ecclesiastical use. The use of an ox horn as a drinking horn on the Bayeux Tapestry is illustrated in Plate 20. To make the horn usable for drinking it must always

Schiedlausky, *op. cit.,* p. 7.

MS. Reg. 2, B.VIII; Wright, *History of Domestic Manners* (London, 1862), p. 162.

Schiedlausky, *op. cit.,* .p. 13.
Arthur von Schneider, *Die Glasgemälde des Badischen Landesmuseums, Carlsruhe* (Freiburg im Breisgau, 1949), Plate 79.

Pepys, *Diary,* October 29, 1663.

MS. Reg. 2, B.VIII reproduced in Wright, *History of Domestic Manners* (London, 1862), fig. 119.

Schiedlausky, *op. cit.,* p. 35.

Household Ordinances, p. 345.

B.G., VI, 28.
Sir Mortimer Wheeler, *Rome beyond the Imperial Frontiers* (London, 1954), pp. 36, 39, 42.
The Sutton Hoo Ship Burial (London, British Museum, 1947), p. 28.
Shetelig, *Scandinavian Archaeology* (London, 1927), p. 208.
T. H. White (ed. and tra.) *The Book of Beasts* (London, 1955), p. 78.
Wheeler, *op. cit.,* p. 86 and Plate XV, B.
Brussels, Musée d'Art et d'Histoire, *L'Art Merovingien* (Brussels, 1954), p. 53 and Plate 36.
Surtees Society *The Life and Miracles of St. Godric.* Vol. 20, Chapter XXXVIII, p. 93.

C. C. Oman, 'English Medieval Drinking Horns', *Connoisseur*, vol. CXIII, March 1944, pp. 20-33.

have had at least a small mount closing the narrow end, but in the later Middle Ages much more elaborate mounts became common. The earlier type is seen in Plate 20; of the later type five English examples are known, two of the fourteenth and three of the fifteenth century.* One of the latter, of about 1450, is shown in Plate 21.

Many other types of drinking vessels were in use, made of various materials in silver-gilt mounts. These were chiefly coconut (Plate 22) and nautilus and other shells (Plate 23). Coconut was believed, towards the end of the Middle Ages, to have medicinal properties, and remained popular as a material for drinking vessels up to the middle of the sixteenth century or even later. The first English reference is in a will of 1259. These were the precursors of the much smaller and more personal wine cup which came into use late in the reign of Elizabeth and of which an example is shown in Plate 24.

Of a character similar to these are two other vessels, the beaker and the tankard. The beaker, at first often of horn and only later of silver, was in use in England by the fourteenth century, and examples dating from all the rest of this period are known. The tankard appears first in a stone relief, probably Roman in date, from Charsada in Gandhara.* The first known European examples are Scandinavian, and though they are similar to the one Silenus holds on the stone relief, it is difficult to believe that there can be any connection between the two. It is supposed that the Scandinavian types influenced the German and the German the English; the earliest dated English example is of 1561, a horn drum mounted in silver-gilt.

I. L. N., February 7, 1959, p. 235.

Medieval drinking vessels seem indeed to have been of many different types made of many different materials. Their variety, in fact, is exceeded only by Rabelais' description of the Oracle of the Bottle at the end of *Pantagruel*:

'First, on one side was to be seen a long train of flagons, leathern bottles, flasks, cans, glass bottles, barrels, nipperkins, pint pots, quart pots, pottles, gallons, old-fashioned semaises (swinging wooden pots, such as those out of which the Germans fill their glasses): these hung on a shady arbour . . . On another were hundreds of sorts of drinking glasses, cups, cisterns, ewers, false cups, bowls, mazers, mugs, jugs, goblets, talboys* and other Bacchic artillery.'*

This use of the word 'talboy' or 'tallboy' is confirmed by a quotation of 1676, given in the *OED* from d'Urfey, 'At Lambs with the Fidles and a Talboy'.
Rabelais, *Works*, ed. by Urquhart and Motteux (London, n.d.), pp. 491-2.

The drinking vessels already mentioned, except for the ox horn and the tankard, were variants of the 'stemmed cup' type. Another popular one is seen at its clearest in the mazer, treated below in the section on wood.

Of the materials used on the table, glass was one which though often decorative, was at the same time purely utilitarian. Later medieval pictures show us glass vessels in use in a great variety of settings; it seems in fact that it is not until the sixteenth century that glass began to acquire its modern status as an 'art form'. Early medieval glass in England was very often an import from abroad; the factory at Chiddingfold in Kent is first heard of in the thirteenth century. That glass was fairly well known by Chaucer's time is implied by the passage from *The Squire's Tale*,

'And others said how strange it was to learn
That glass is made out of the ash of fern
Though bearing no resemblances to glass
But being used to this they let it pass.'*

Chaucer, *Canterbury Tales* (London, 1951), p. 420.

Glass was prized and perhaps the more valued in that it would never have to be surrendered for melting down in times of need, but utilitarian in type though fragile and to be treated with care. *The Young Scholar's Paradise*, one of the books of instruction, urges that:

'Let glasses be scoured in country guise
With salt and fair water and ever devise
The place most convenient where they may stand,
The safest from breaking and nearest at hand.'*

Edith Rickert, *The Babees Book* (London, 1908), p. 162.

In other countries, however, glass was obviously considered of no great value, and treated accordingly.

Of the other materials mentioned, earthenware jugs (Plates 27a, 27b) were probably in use in the Hall for washing, for wine, for ale, and perhaps for soup. Other vessels of earthenware, such as the soup bowl in Plate 25, were in use on the table as well. The earthenware wine jars of the Marriage Feast at Cana are shown in Plate 4. Earthenware jugs are referred to by the *Ménagier* as having been in use in the kitchen: 'Three large earthenware pots for wine, large earthenware pot for potage . . .'*

Eileen Power (ed.), *The Goodman of Paris* (London, 1928), p. 242.

This use of pottery as a material for containing wine finds parallels in England. The earliest known type of English wine container (Plate 26a) is a baluster-shaped vessel with a large handle and a very heavy foot. In the two known examples* the upper part of the body is covered with a dark green glaze, and may be dated about 1300. Later vessels are of two types, those intended to stand on a table and those meant to be carried. An example

One of these is in the Royal Ontario Museum, the other in the Glaisher Collection at Cambridge. It is published in Rackham, *Catalogue of the Glaisher Collection of Pottery and Porcelain . . .*, 1935, 2, Plate 1.

of the former (Plate 26b) has a rather globular body, a short neck, and small handle. The best known example of this group is the 'Bellarmine' jug; this has a slightly larger body and a longer vertical neck, at the base of which is a raised representation of a bearded face, believed to have been originally a caricature of Cardinal Bellarmine. Other wine vessels have lugs in various forms to hold a cord for carrying. The best known of these is the 'Pilgrim Bottle'; a late example of English slipware is shown on Plate 26c

Pottery was used for drinking as well as storage. What may have been a wine cup of the sixteenth century is shown in Plate 26b, but with these early drinking vessels it is never possible to be certain about the use.

Pewter vessels are shown in a number of paintings of the fifteenth and

Plate 31. Set of small trenchers with box, sycamore. Diameter of trenchers 4⅞", of box 5⅛". English, about 1600. Toronto, Royal Ontario Museum.

R. Edwards, *Early Conversation Pictures* (London, 1954), Plates 5, 8, 14, 19, 46, 47.

H. Swarzenski, *Monuments of Romanesque Art*, 1955, Plate 71.

Eileen Power (ed.), *The Goodman of Paris* (London, 1928), pp. 242, 246.

Manners and Household Expenses, p. 279.

John Fenn (ed.) (re-ed. by Mrs. Archer-Hind) *The Paston Letters* (London, 1951), vol. I, pp. 216-17, letter 202.

Household Ordinances, p. 196.

Ibid., p. 195.

Oliver Baker, *Black Jacks and Leather Bottells* (London, 1921) *passim*.

Chaucer, *Canterbury Tales* (London, 1951) p. 285.

Rabelais, *Works*, ed. by Urquhart and Motteux (London, n.d.), p. 120.

Eileen Power (ed.), *The Goodman of Paris* (London, 1928), pp. 242, 246.

Manners and Household Expenses, pp. 192-3, 527.

Household Ordinances, p. 285.

Wright, *History of Domestic Manners* (London, 1862), p. 449.

Furnivall, *op. cit.*, p. 68.

Ibid., p. 369.

Stenton, *The Bayeux Tapestry* (London, 1957), Plate 49.

Furnivall, *op. cit.*, p. 343.

sixteenth centuries;* small flat pewter plates are shown at a much earlier date in a manuscript of St. Germain of about 1050.* The *Ménagier* refers several times to large sets: 'The pewter vessels; to wit ten dozen bowls, six dozen small dishes, two dozen and a half large dishes, eight quart (pots), two dozen pint (pots), two alms dishes.'* Sets of pewter vessels are mentioned in the Howard Accounts,* and a contemporary reference is in a letter of Margaret Paston to her husband, written early in the reign of Edward IV;* pewter vessels are referred to in a summary list of expenses of the 'Squillery' in the Eltham Ordinances of 1526.* The popularity of pewter throughout the latter part of the period in many different countries cannot be over-estimated. The type of large platter of which a late example is shown in Plate 28 must indeed have been one of the commoner utensils.

Leather is not referred to in any of the earlier written sources, but is mentioned in the Eltham Ordinances.* The character of the vessels that remain suggests that the fashion for it was not one ever followed by the richer classes of society. Towards the end of the period it had various different uses in England. It was used in the kitchen fairly commonly, and a jug, or a 'black jack',* perhaps of the seventeenth century, is shown in Plate 29a. Also shown in Plate 29b is a leather tankard, rather tall and narrow, with a lining of silver.

Wood was in common use. As Chaucer's Wife of Bath says,

'For in a noble household, we are told
Not every dish and vessel's made of gold,
Some are of wood, yet earn their Master's praise.'*

Mazer wood, a generic term for close-grained woods such as alder, maple and cherry, was in use for drinking vessels. The mazer was a quite common shallow drinking vessel, normally without a stem, and a number of these, many in silver mounts, are in existence; Rabelais, describing one character, says 'His eyes are as red as a mazer made of an alder tree.'* It seems that the use of such a cup was on the whole a habit belonging to a less exalted rank in society than the use of stemmed drinking vessels, though a late stemmed cup of wood is shown in Plate 30. This may be implied by the quotation from Chaucer's Wife of Bath, and seems also to be the implication of the passage from Shakespeare's *Richard II*, III. iii where in his speech of renunciation the King says 'I'll give . . . my figured goblets for a dish of wood.' Wooden basins and spoons are referred to by the *Ménagier* as being used in both Hall and kitchen.* In the fifteenth century various wooden vessels are mentioned in the Howard Accounts.* 'Silver pots, jacks and wooden cups' are referred to in Queen Elizabeth's Household Book, 1601.* A sixteenth century carving in Kirby Thorpe church in Yorkshire shows a cook washing up a number of large dishes, presumably of wood or pewter, over a cauldron.* An example of the type appears on the table in Plate 4.

After the main courses of the medieval dinner, what we would now call a dessert was often served. 'If your Lord will have any conceits after dinner, as apples, nuts or cream . . .', says Hugh Rhodes in the *Book of Nurture;* we also hear of fruit and cheese being eaten.* The subject of what happened after this last course was over is one on which the books of instruction are neither unanimous nor clear, since not all of them follow the dinner through to the end. As far as we can make out, the first event that took place was the washing of hands. At the end of the meal this was done sitting down, the basin, ewer and towel being brought to the diner; a figure kneeling beside the Bishop on the Bayeux Tapestry carries a ewer and basin,* and is clearly ready for the washing of hands at the end of the meal. The practice is referred to in Seager's *School of Virtue:*

'The basin and ewer to the table then bring
In place convenient their pleasure abiding
When thou should see them ready to wash
The ewer take up and be not too rashe
In pouring out water more than will suffice. *

A similar picture is given by Hugh Rhodes's *Book of Nurture*

'If your Master's habit is to wash at the table, have a clean towel on the table cloth and put down the basin and ewer before him. When he is done take them away.'*

Furnivall, *op. cit.*, p. 68.

There is another passage on this subject in *For to Serve a Lord*.*

Ibid., p. 371.

Grace was then said, and at this point the written sources seem to divide into two groups. One maintains that the diners stayed at the table, which was completely cleared, a drinking vessel being placed before each diner. This is the version given, for instance, by *For to Serve a Lord*. On the other hand, the *Boke of Curtasye* and others maintain that after the removal of the table cloths and the washing of hands, grace is said and the table is removed by lowering the top onto the floor and taking away both it and the trestles.*

Ibid., p. 326.

The guests were then free to leave the Hall and to retire to the Chamber for a rest, and *For to Serve a Lord* says a fire is to be lit there during the winter and if there is a bed there it is to be covered in summer with pillows and sheets 'in case that they will rest'.* A light meal was then served, often fruit (cherries and apples in summer) and cream (perhaps clotted); in winter 'green ginger comfits with such things as winter requireth' replaced them. It must have been on an occasion such as this that the small wooden trenchers that came into fashion during the sixteenth century were used.*

Ibid., p. 370-5.

Both oval and rectangular trenchers of this kind are known, but most are round, about five inches in diameter, very thin, and made in sets of twelve with a special box. One side was left plain and the other painted with scenes, emblems or inscriptions, and it is suggested that the meal was eaten off the plain side and that when the diner had finished eating he turned over the trencher so as to see the decoration. A number of sets remain today; in many of them each trencher has a floral or emblematic painting, a couplet of verses, and sometimes a text. This is often taken from Coverdale's translation of the Bible (Plate 31).

G. Brett, 'Trenchers', *Annual. Art and Archeology Division, The Royal Ontario Museum. University of Toronto*, 1962, p. 23f.

The later stages of the dinner are not normally referred to in our sources. Indeed, almost the only description is that given by the *Ménagier*, who visualizes a quick, almost abrupt ending: 'Wine and spices are the Sally-forth. Wash, grace, and go to the Withdrawing Room, and the servants dine and immediately afterwards serve wine and spices. And so farewell.'*

Eileen Power (ed.), *The Goodman of Paris* (London, 1928), p. 238.

Part 2

1660-1900

Sources of information

These—the vessels and implements, the pictorial information and the literary information—are basically the same as those discussed in Part I, but each has altered in character and their relative importance has changed. The first has lost the enormous variety of material which distinguished it in the earlier period: this early variety has been replaced by three materials only, metal, glass and pottery. Of these, metal (usually silver or an imitation of it) is quite often mentioned when used, glass almost always is, pottery despite quite extensive use is hardly ever mentioned before about 1850. Each of these has to be approached differently since each has made its own contribution to the table settings of this period.

Among the metals, pewter, bronze and latten have lost much or all their early importance, and the word *metal* used here is an intentionally general one covering silver, which for long was much the most popular, and all its modern imitations. The most important of these are Sheffield plate (copper overlaid on both sides by sheets of silver; invented in 1743), Britannia metal (an alloy of tin, antimony and copper, dating from the late eighteenth century), German silver (an alloy of copper, zinc and nickel dating from 1830) and the various types of electro-plated nickel developed by members of the Elkington family of Birmingham in the early 1840's.*

The range of objects made for the table in silver, later in Sheffield plate and much later in the other imitation materials increased steadily until after 1800. The use of silver itself seems to have reached its highest level about that date. The victories in the Revolutionary and Napoleonic Wars had begun by 1805 to produce a great outburst of national pride, and it was in keeping both with this and with the prevailing Neoclassical style that there grew up a fashion for heavy, massive and elaborate silver on the table.

The Regency of the Prince of Wales saw the currency of a style which lasted until 1825, if not 1830. In a sense it is the beginning of the end, for it was the last period to witness at the same time both the rule of the old aristocracy, often ready to spend large sums on celebrations, and the need to celebrate a number of really striking national victories. With the rise of the middle classes the use of silver in private households, which had increased steadily from about 1660, began to be replaced by imitation materials.

The sixteenth and seventeenth centuries stand out as the first period when *glass* was a widely valued possession. The great event in its late medieval history in Europe was the Venetian invention of the wine glass;* but it was long before we can be sure that this was used in England. The great event in its modern history was the English seventeenth century discovery of lead glass, produced by the addition of litharge (one of the oxides of lead) to the earlier ingredients. After the Restoration there grew up a multiplicity of forms and shapes in glass: Plates 60 and 61 show types of wine glass in use at this time.

Pottery is used in much the same general way as *metal*. It covers earthenware and stoneware, the latter first made in England in the seventeenth century, porcelain, made in England since 1743, and the material which since the late nineteenth century has been known as 'bone china'. This seems to have been originally a shopkeeper's phrase, and dates from the 1880's or 90's, though the word 'china' has been used since the sixteenth century to signify all forms of clay material. The greatest event in the history of pottery used for the table was the introduction during the eighteenth century of the *Service*—the breakfast service, the dinner service, the tea service—and there are many remains of large services in households today.

Second is the pictorial evidence. Plates 32 and 33 show scenes which date before 1660, but which are reproduced at this point because they show an early stage in the development of the form of service typical of the modern period. Plate 32 shows James I and Henry Prince of Wales dining with (supposedly) the Spanish Ambassador; a Spanish marriage was proposed for Prince Henry, who died in 1612. The engraving, however, is much later than the scene it shows. It is taken from an unidentified Spanish book, and

Shirley Bury, in *Connoisseur Period Guide: Early Victorian* (London, 1958), p. 69f.

Francis Buckley, *History of Old English Glass* (London, 1925), chapters 5, 7, 8 and 9.

probably belongs to the years about 1700; it may be a close, even an exact, copy of a much earlier scene. Even as late as this it is a contemporary record of this form of service. Earlier than this, and contemporary with the event it shows, is a painting by the Dutch artist Houckgeest (1600-1661) showing Charles I at dinner (Plate 33). Turning to the eighteenth century we find that Conversation Piece paintings pay attention to tea drinking but not to the eating of any other meal. Still Life paintings of dinner table scenes exist, but there is very little work in this *genre* by English artists. It is not until the coming of the Naturalism of the later eighteenth and nineteenth century schools of English painting and the growth of the Italian school of *Caricatura* as practised in England (Plates 34 and 35) that dinner table scenes begin to be anything other than very rare. The cartoonist Richard Doyle is one of the exceptions to this rule (Plate 36). Even in the twentieth century, dinner table scenes are rare.

Third is the literary evidence, which until about 1760 is uncommon, but since then has been as large in bulk as the pictorial was small. Literary sources differ from their predecessors just as do both the objects used at the table and the pictorial evidence. The books concerned fall into four special sections of which the first two are the work of practising cooks. The earliest dealt with in detail here is Elizabeth Smith, *The Compleat Housewife*, 1727, a book treating the kitchen along with the rest of the household. It is one of a group of which much the most prominent example is Mrs. Beeton's famous *Book of Household Management*, 1861, which has been re-edited and reprinted many times. Second is the book dealing only with the kitchen. An eighteenth century example dealt with here in detail is *The Art of Cooking Made Plain and Easy*, published anonymously in 1747 and usually attributed to Mrs. Hannah Glasse. Third is a type of book which, with the appearance of Dr. Kitchiner's *Apicius Redivivus, or The Cook's Oracle*, 1817 in England and Brillat-Savarin's *La Physiologie du Goût*, 1825 in France has passed the other two in popularity. It is a book written not by a cook but by an epicure, and deals not with the proper preparation of food but more generally with food (and sometimes drink also), and with the proper manner and pleasures of its consumption. Many modern epicures have written in the vein of Dr. Kitchiner and Brillat-Savarin, and have refined and made more delicate the whole subject of Food, so that it became in the nineteenth century 'The Art of Dining', as Abraham Hayward called it. The last group consists of novels, biographies, letters and books of reminiscences, many of which contain incidental references to this subject.

Setting and furniture

The Hall and the Chamber were the usual settings for medieval meals. Towards the end of the early period the Hall declined in importance and finally became the Entrance Hall of modern times. The Chamber was the forerunner of the Drawing Room, and as the subdivision of space increased it became the custom to set aside a special room for eating meals. This came to be known as either an 'eating room' or a 'dining room'. The former phrase is used by the elderly and old-fashioned General Tilney in Chapter 20 of Jane Austen's *Northanger Abbey*, written, though not published, in 1798. The latter phrase is first recorded in 1601, and there are other instances in both the seventeenth and eighteenth centuries. We do not know why 'dining room' was preferred, but the reason may be that it was held to be less descriptive and therefore more suitable.

A different kind of meal, which we must equally consider, is that eaten out-of-doors. Whereas in England all periods up to about 1750 regarded eating out-of-doors as an unpleasant necessity at best, it has since then been elevated to an event of great importance.* Outdoor meals in England have been of two kinds. One is probably derived from the *fête champêtre* of France, which was known well enough in England to be referred to by Sheridan in *The School for Scandal* (II. i), where Sir Peter Teazle addresses Lady Teazle

G. Grigson, *Country Life*, August 20, 1959, p. 54f, deals with the early history in several different countries.

'. . . to spend enough money to furnish your dressing room with flowers in winter as would suffice to turn the Pantheon into a greenhouse, or to give a *fête champêtre* at Christmas'. It is perhaps the origin of the breakfast given by by Mrs. Leo Hunter in the *Pickwick Papers*, Chapter 15. The other is the Picnic. This is a word thought to be of seventeenth century origin, possibly derived from the French. It very soon came into use in almost all European languages, and appears in one of the letters of Lord Chesterfield written in

Plate 32. Engraving of a Dinner of James I, Henry Prince of Wales (d. 1612) and (probably) the Spanish Ambassador. Taken from an unidentified Spanish book, about 1700.

1748. Though it is sometimes referred to in English writing during the eighteenth century, such references are all to events happening in Europe, and the picnic does not seem to have become an English institution until about 1800. The word is defined in the *OED* as 'originally a social entertainment in which each person contributed a share . . . [now] a pleasure party to some spot in the country for a meal out-of-doors.' This meal has sometimes been substantial rather than elegant, like the meals provided by Old Wardle both at the Rochester Review in Chapter 4 and at the shooting party in Chapter 19 of *The Pickwick Papers*; sometimes very elaborate, resembling the 'picnic for forty' for which Mrs. Beeton, writing about 1860, suggests a bill of fare. This bill of fare, to the modern reader, is so extraordinary and so much out of keeping with what a picnic is today, that it is included here:

Bill of Fare for a Picnic for 40 Persons
'A joint of cold roast beef, a joint of cold boiled beef, 2 ribs of lamb, 2 shoulders of lamb, 4 roast fowls, 2 roast ducks, 1 ham, 1 tongue, 2 veal-and-ham pies, 2 pigeon pies, 6 medium-sized lobsters, 1 piece of collared calf's head, 18 lettuces, 6 baskets of salad, 6 cucumbers.

Plate 33. Painting 'Charles I at Dinner' by Gerard Houckgeest (1600-1661). Reproduced by Gracious Permission of Her Majesty Queen Elizabeth II.

'Stewed fruit well sweetened, and put into glass bottles well corked; 3 or 4 dozen plain pastry biscuits to eat with the stewed fruit, 2 dozen fruit turnovers, 4 dozen cheesecakes, 2 cold cabinet puddings in moulds, 2 blancmanges in moulds, a few jam puffs, 1 large cold Christmas plum-pudding (this must be good), a few baskets of fresh fruit, 3 dozen plain biscuits, a piece of cheese, 6 lbs of butter (this, of course, includes the butter for tea), 4 quartern loaves of household bread, 3 dozen rolls, 6 loaves of tin bread (for

tea), 2 plain plum cakes, 2 pound cakes, 2 sponge cakes, a tin of mixed biscuits, ½ lb of tea. Coffee is not suitable for a picnic, being difficult to make. 'Things not to be forgotten at a Picnic; a stick of horseradish, a bottle of mint sauce well corked, a bottle of salad dressing, a bottle of vinegar, made mustard, pepper, salt, good oil, and pounded sugar. If it can be managed take a little ice. It is scarcely necessary to say that plates, tumblers, wine-glasses, knives, forks and spoons must not be forgotten; as also teacups and saucers, 3 or 4 teapots, some lump sugar, and milk, if this last-named article cannot be obtained in the neighbourhood. Take 3 corkscrews.
'Beverages:- 3 dozen quart bottles of ale, packed in hampers; ginger-beer, soda-water, and lemonade, of each 2 dozen bottles; 6 bottles of sherry, 6 bottles of claret, champagne *à discretion*, and any other light wine that may be preferred, and 2 bottles of brandy. Water can usually be obtained, so it is useless to take it.'*

Our standards today are not normally, however, on Mrs. Beeton's high level.

When we turn from the setting of the meal to the furniture used in the dining room, we find it far more varied than before. The first piece to be considered is the dining table. The old style of table made of boards laid on trestles went out of fashion completely during the sixteenth century, and dining tables made since then have had either four corner legs, or, in later examples, a central pedestal: in both types the top and the supports are permanently fixed together. Among the changes that occurred in English furniture about the time of the Restoration was the disappearance of the ponderous 'shuffle board' type of table, and its replacement by one of the variants of the type of dining table Samuel Pepys saw at the Lord Treasurer's '. . . one pretty piece of household stuff, as the Company increaseth, to put a larger leaf upon an ovall table'.* This extendable table with a half circle

Plate 34. Coffee House Scene, by Thomas Rowlandson (1756-1827).

Mrs. Beeton, *Book of Household Management*, London, 1861, p. 1000.

Diary, 28th May, 1665.

Plate 35. *My Table at Home, from Alexis Soyer,*
The Gastronomic Regenerator, 1848.

R. Edwards, *Dictionary of English Furniture*,
2nd ed., 1954, s.v. 'Tables, Side', p. 282 and
fig. 28f.

John Swarbrick (ed.), *The Works in Architec-
ture of Robert and James Adam* (Chicago, 1959),
Plates 22 and 31.

at each end, the centre formed of boards held in position by clamps, remained popular throughout the seventeenth and eighteenth centuries. Whether the ends are half round or rectangular, the difficulty of this type of table is the number of legs it involves, and the consequent difficulty of seating a large company. About 1800 the separate legs were replaced by the 'pedestal and claw' type of central support.

The picture is different as it concerns the side table. The Court Cupboard went out of use during the seventeenth century, to be replaced either by the Console Table without legs, with a framework nailed to the wall, or by the type of much broader and squarer table which Chippendale calls 'Sideboard Table'. This large and decorative side table was most in use during the first half of the eighteenth century, and is best known in examples often attributed to William Kent, and to be dated between 1730 and 1740.* Both it and the console table came about 1700 to be covered with thick marble slabs. It must be supposed that the presence of the slabs was due in the first place to the use of the table in the dining room because they would be more or less impervious to the splashes and spatters of serving. We cannot help thinking that such tables were sometimes used at this time for the very elaborate arrangement of dishes visualized in the Plates to Mrs. Smith's book among others: two of these are shown in Plates 39 and 40. Of a rather later date are the large sideboards in three pieces, a central table with a tall urn on a pedestal at each end. This urn, at first a purely decorative feature, was originally made of stone. Such an urn appears in John Vardy, *Some Furniture Designs of . . . Mr. William Kent*, 1740, and there is an example (probaby not of stone) in Robert Adam's designs for Syon House of the early 1760's.* Also in the designs for Syon House we find the side table with the urn on a pedestal at each end, together forming one unit. As time progressed the urns were transformed into knife boxes, the earlier separate knife box being

91

discarded, while the pedestals were pressed into service as containers for hot water. A piece which combined the table and the pedestals, here without urns, appears in the furniture designs of Thomas Shearer in 1788.* Such a composite piece and the type with the three separate units appear side by side in the furniture design books of the first quarter of the nineteenth century.* The former became the typical early Victorian sideboard, and as such was the object of much decoration and elaboration. A plainer type of sideboard began to become usual during the 1860's, and was supplemented and later superseded by smaller and more movable kinds.

The Console Table remained popular throughout the eighteenth century. In the earlier examples the narrow top, though fixed to the wall, is actually supported by the fanciful shapes below it, but towards the end of the century the connection between the two parts tends to disappear and the fanciful shapes below are only decorative and do not support the table top. The console table is a common feature of the design books of the middle and latter part of the eighteenth century, but makes its last appearance in George Smith's *Designs for Household Furniture*, 1808.

There is little that can be said about seating furniture intended specially for the dining room. The bench and the stool had begun to give way to the chair by about 1600. So far as the English dining room is concerned, the process seems to have been almost complete by the time of the Restoration. It is normally impossible to distinguish a side chair made for a dining room from a side chair made for a sitting room.

The nineteenth century added little to this repertory of forms, and its additions lie mainly in the development of existing types rather than in the invention of new ones. There were new kinds of sideboards, as has been pointed out; equally important was a piece introduced towards the end of the century, the Butler's Tray. This was an oval tray, the sides and ends of which could be turned up on hinges so as to enclose a rectangular space in the centre. All four sides of this have holes for carrying. The Butler's Tray was intended to make easier the process of laying the table for dinner with

Furniture Designs from the Cabinet-Maker's London Book of Prices, 1788 (reprint, London, 1962), Plate 6.

Sheraton, *The Cabinet Dictionary*, 1803, Plate 72 (one continuous piece, a cupboard at each end and open legs below); George Smith, *Designs for Household Furniture*, 1808, Plates 92, 93 (the three-piece sideboard) cp. Plate 94 (table with rounded front and low raised section at each end), Plate 95 (continuous type with cupboard at each end and raised part above each); George Smith, *Cabinet-Maker and Upholsterer's Guide*, 1826, Plate IV (three-piece type), cp. Plate LXXV (continuous type with cupboard at each end and raised part above each).

Plate 36. A State Party by Richard Doyle, from 'A Bird's Eye View of Society', The Cornhill Magazine, 1861.

Plate 37. *Table of the Wealthy, from Alexis Soyer*, The Gastronomic Regenerator, 1848.

Plate 38. *Mr. Jorrocks' Hunt Breakfast, from a lithograph by Henry Alken* (1774-1850).

a large number of small objects, many of them breakable. It would stand on a high trestle which raised it three feet, or three feet six inches above the level of the floor. The Butler's Tray, like the butler himself, is now rather a thing of the past, but examples of the tray without the trestle that once supported it, are sometimes seen.

Meals of the day

The three meals a day normally eaten during the later Middle Ages—an early breakfast, a dinner at some time before midday, and supper at about 6 p.m.—were replaced in this period by the four normally eaten today—breakfast, luncheon or dinner, afternoon tea, and dinner or supper—while the four have altered greatly in arrangement and time. These changes are one small aspect of the move away from the aristocratic civilization inherited and transmitted with little change by the Middle Ages, which withstood all challenges throughout Western Europe until the outbreak of the French Revolution in 1789. In England it lasted into the nineteenth century, and there was no outward change there until the events which led up to and accompanied the Reform Bill of 1832 that symbolized the beginning of the middle class civilization of the Victorians. In the present context, it was a change from a time when the upper classes did not in general do regular daily work, to one in which such work in an office or factory is the general rule. This change had an effect on the hours when meals were served.

Breakfast, like the other meals, has altered both in time and size. We know little of the hour at which breakfast was eaten at the beginning of this period and have to depend on our judgement of what is likely. Pepys tells us in his *Diary* that he sometimes rose 'betimes' and sometimes 'very betimes'. The meaning of the first of these phrases is never given, but the second is identified as meaning 4 a.m. If he followed the usual practice of the period in not breakfasting until some hours after rising, we can assume that his breakfast hour was about 6 or 7 a.m., hardly later. We may note in passing that this habit was similar to that followed much later by Anthony Trollope. Trollope tells us in his autobiography that he rose at 5 and worked at his writing for three hours 'before dressing for breakfast'.* By the end of the eighteenth century the usual hour had slipped to 10 o'clock, and Maria Josepha Holroyd, Lord Sheffield's daughter, then aged sixteen, remarks in a letter of 1786 that she rose at 8, walked out at 9, and had breakfast at 10.* Since then, for the reasons just given, the tendency of breakfast has been to move backwards against the clock, rather than forward with it as the other meals have done. Between 8 and 9 o'clock seems to have been a common hour for a hundred years or more.

Breakfast varies enormously, by individual taste. It is described by the Victorian cartoonist Richard Doyle in *A Bird's Eye View of Society*, as 'the pleasantest meal of the day, because no one is conceited before lunch time'.* A different view is taken by the 1880 editor of Mrs. Beeton, who says

'Our advice is, eat as good a breakfast as you can; it is a foundation both mentally and bodily for health during the day.'*

In the eighteenth century a light breakfast is the type most commonly recorded. It is described by La Rochefoucauld in *Mélanges sur l'Angleterre*, 1784.

'Throughout England it is the custom to breakfast together, the meal resembling a dinner or a supper in France . . . Breakfast consists of tea and bread and butter in various forms. In the house of the rich you have coffee, chocolate and so on. The morning papers are on the table and those who want to do so read them during breakfast, so the conversation is not of a lively nature.'*

A slightly larger meal—we should perhaps remember that both those who ate it were starting on a journey—is described by Jane Austen in *Mansfield Park*, 1814. This speaks of the remnants of breakfast as consisting of 'the cold pork bones and mustard on her [Fanny Price's] brother's plate, and the broken egg shells on Mr. Crawford's'.* A far more solid meal is described by Trollope in the Rectory at Plumstead Episcopi in Chapter 8 of *The Warden*, 1855. Such a meal is recommended by the Reverend Dr. Folliott in

Plate 39. *Plan for the lay-out of dishes on a table, from Elizabeth Smith,* The Compleat Housewife, 1727.

A. Trollope, *An Autobiography* (London, 1883), p. 103.

Quoted by Arnold Palmer, *Movable Feasts* (London, 1952), p. 17. The first part of this chapter, especially the passages dealing with the changes in the hour of dinner, owes much to this book.

Cornhill Magazine, Vol. III, 1861, p. 497f.

Book of Household Management, 1880 ed., p. 1237.

La Rochefoucauld, *Mélanges sur L'Angleterre* (*A Frenchman in England*), 1784, p. 28.

Jane Austen, *Mansfield Park*, 1814, chapter XXIX.

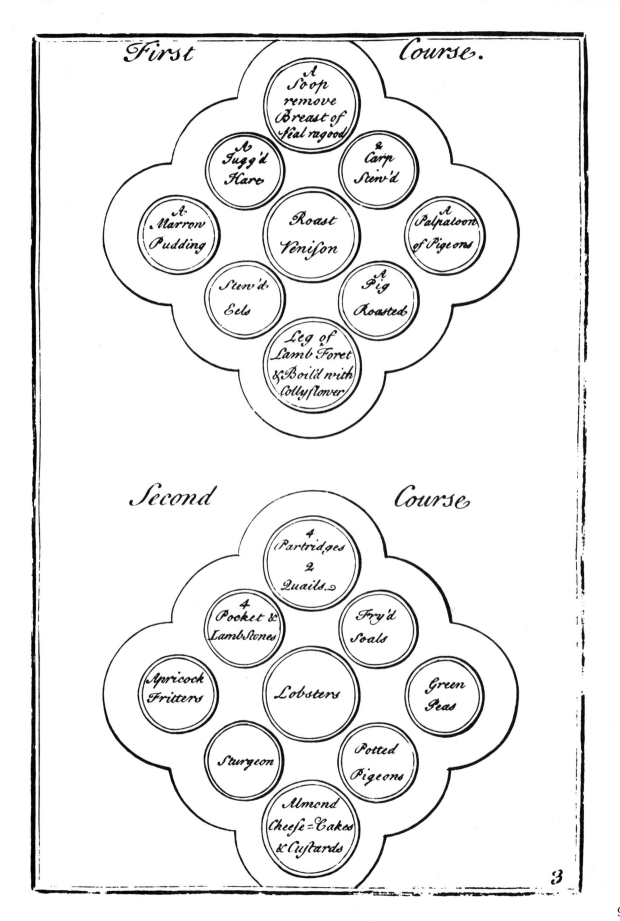

First Course.

A Soop remove Breast of Veal ragood

A Jugg'd Hare

2 Carp Stew'd

A Marrow Pudding

Roast Venison

A Palpatoon of Pigeons

Stew'd Eels

A Pig Roasted

Leg of Lamb Foret & Boil'd with Collyflower

Second Course

4 Partridges 2 Quails

4 Pocket & Lamb Stones

Fry'd Soals

Apricock Fritters

Lobsters

Green Peas

Sturgeon

Potted Pigeons

Almond Cheese=Cakes & Custards

3

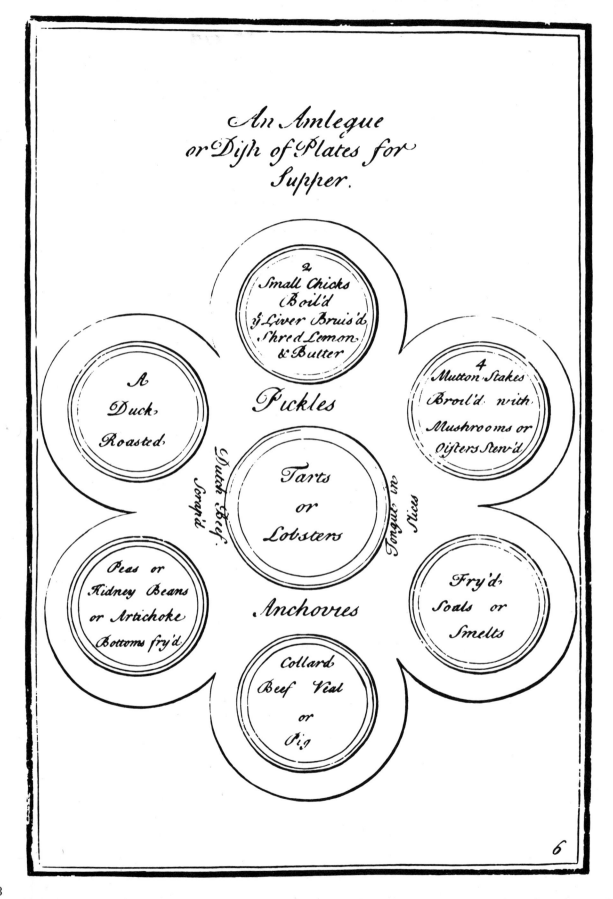

An Amlegue
or Dish of Plates for
Supper.

2
Small Chicks
Boil'd
ye Liver Bruis'd
Shred Lemon
& Butter

Pickles

A
Duck
Roasted

4
Mutton Stakes
Broil'd with
Mushrooms or
Oisters Stew'd

Dutch Beef
Scrap'd

Tarts
or
Lobsters

Tongue in
Slices

Peas or
Kidney Beans
or Artichoke
Bottoms fry'd

Anchovies

Fry'd
Soals or
Smelts

Collard
Beef Veal
or
Pig

6

Plate 40. *Plan for the lay-out of dishes on a table, from Elizabeth Smith*, The Compleat House-wife, 1727.

T. L. Peacock's mock-Gothic novel *Crotchet Castle*, 1831.

'The divine took his seat at the breakfast table, and began to compose his spirits by the gentle sedative of a large cup of tea, the demulcent of a well-buttered muffin, and the tonic of a small lobster.

THE REV. DR. FOLLIOTT. You are a man of taste, Mr. Crotchet. A man of taste is seen at once in the array of his breakfast-table. It is the foot of Hercules, the far-shining face of the great work, according to Pindar's doctrine: ἀρχομένου ἔργου, πρόσωπον χρὴ θέμεν τηλαυγές. The breakfast is the πρόσωπον of the great work of the day. Chocolate, coffee, tea, cream, eggs, ham, tongue, cold fowl—all these are good, and bespeak good knowledge in him who sets them forth: but the touchstone is fish: anchovy is the first step, prawns and shrimps the second; and I laud him who reaches even to these: potted char and lampreys are the third, and a fine stretch of progression; but lobster is, indeed, matter for a May morning, and demands a rare combination of knowledge and virtue in him who sets it forth.

MR. MAC‧QUEDY. Well, sir, and what say you to a fine fresh trout, hot and dry, in a napkin? or a herring out of the water into the frying pan, on the shore of Loch Fyne?

THE REV. DR. FOLLIOTT. Sir, I say every nation has some eximious virtue; and your country is pre-eminent in the glory of fish for breakfast. We have much to learn from you in that line at any rate.'*

T. L. Peacock, *Crotchet Castle*, 1831, Chapter II.

The eating of fish, though more normally of trout than of lobster, became a regular feature of the English breakfast during the nineteenth century. The popularity of sole seems to be an aspect of this, and so is the modern vogue for the kipper, which has been in use for several hundred years. The noun Kipper is given two meanings in the *OED*: 'a male salmon or sea trout during the spawning season', and 'a cured fish, by smoking' (today it is normally a herring). There are late medieval uses of it, for instance in the Durham Account Book, though this does not mention drying or curing. Defoe, in the *Tour of Great Britain*, published in 1769 but written many years earlier, speaks of 'preserving salmon by making it into what they call kipper: this is done by . . . drying it before a fire'.* In 1837 Michael Donovan notes 'Some people now give a kipper a peculiar taste . . . carefully smoking with peat-reek or the reek of juniper bushes.'* Considering how long herrings have been a popular article of diet in England, it is perhaps surprising at what a late date the kipper makes its appearance in books of any kind, but having done so it became and has remained popular indeed.

Defoe, *Tour of Great Britain*, 1769, III, p. 336.

Donovan, *Domestic Economy*, 1837, II, p. 231.

In one important respect the Victorian breakfast seems to mark a retreat. The variety of meat and game dishes suggested in the early editions of Mrs. Beeton began to give way to the egg dishes she mentions, which started as a supplement and often became a replacement—boiled, fried or poached eggs, sometimes with bacon. Bacon and eggs are listed together at a much earlier date*, but it is somewhat problematical just what is meant, and the entry seems to have no connection with the later appearance of the dish. With most of Mrs. Beeton's recipes, as with the earlier forerunners, there is no special connection with breakfast alone; many are described as 'breakfast or supper dishes', or even 'breakfast, luncheon or supper dishes'. In the 1890's Sherlock Holmes and Dr. Watson are recorded as breakfasting off curried chicken, ham and eggs, tea and coffee;* in another story Holmes smokes a before-breakfast pipe while Watson is seeing a patient, and then orders fresh rashers and eggs;* elsewhere Watson points at something with his eggspoon at breakfast.* In the 1880 edition of Mrs. Beeton, bacon and eggs are 'a standard' dish; in 1887 they are 'a national standard' dish. They may still be so described.

J. C. Drummond, *The Englishman's Food*, 2nd edition, 1954, p. 51.

Conan Doyle, *The Naval Treaty*, 1893.

Conan Doyle, *The Engineer's Thumb*, 1892.
Conan Doyle, *A Study in Scarlet*, 1887.

Of the other breakfast foods, porridge and toast must be mentioned here. The breakfast sausage deserves mention but cannot receive it, since although sausages seem to have existed at least since the days of Apicius, there is too

BILLS OF FARE.

◆◆

JANUARY.

2013.—DINNER FOR 18 PERSONS.

First Course.

Mock Turtle Soup,
removed by
Cod's Head and Shoulders.

Stewed Eels.

Tray of
Flowers.

Red Mullet.

Clear Oxtail Soup,
removed by
Fried Filleted Soles.

Entrées.

Riz de Veau aux
Tomatos.

Ragoût of
Lobster.

Tray of
Flowers.

Cotelettes de Porc
à la Robert.

Poulet a la Marengo.

Second Course.

Roast Turkey.

Pigeon Pie.

Boiled Turkey and
Celery Sauce.

Tray of
Flowers.

Boiled Ham.

Tongue, garnished.

Saddle of Mutton.

Third Course.

Charlotte
à la Parisienne.

Pheasants,
removed by
Plum-pudding.

Apricot-Jam
Tartlets.

Jelly.

Cream.

Tray of
Flowers.

Cream.

Jelly.

Mince
Pies.

Maids
of Honour.

Snipes,
removed by
Pommes à la Condé.

We have given above the plan for placing the various dishes of the 1st
Course, Entrées, 2nd Course, and 3rd Course. Following this will be found
bills of fare for smaller parties; and it will be readily seen, by studying the
above arrangement of dishes, how to place a less number for the more limited
company. Several *menus* for dinners *à la Russe*, are also included in the present
chapter.

Plate 41. *Page 1 of the chapter 'Bills of Fare',
from Mrs. Beeton,* Book of Household
Management, *1861.*

little really useful evidence about them to justify a mention. 'Porridge' in
something like its present meaning seems to date from the sixteenth century.
There are many references to it at this early date, but it can hardly have
been considered worthy of note, since no cookery books of this or later periods
seem even to mention it. It is an English belief that porridge has always
been a popular dish in Scotland. Dr. Johnson defines oats in *The Dictionary,*
1755, as 'a grain which in England is generally given to horses, but in
Scotland supports the people'. It seems possible that the Highland Revival
brought about by the fondness for Balmoral shown by Queen Victoria and
the Prince Consort may have helped to provoke an increase in porridge eating.

Toast must be almost as old as the eating of bread, and is referred to in the
earliest English cookery books. The first more detailed description seems to
be that of the Prussian pastor Carl Philipp Moritz, who visited England in
1782, and who remarks

C. P. Moritz, *Travels in England in 1782,*
letter of 5th June.

'The slices of bread and butter, which they give you with your tea, are as
thin as poppy leaves. But there is another kind of bread and butter usually
eaten with tea, which is toasted by the fire and is incomparably good. You
take one slice after the other and hold it to the fire on a fork till the butter is
melted, so that it penetrates a number of slices all at once: this is called *toast.*'*

Plate 42. *Cup, silver (the cover missing). Ht.
3 3/16". London, 1690, possibly by Samuel Dell.
Toronto, Royal Ontario Museum.*

The usual drinks at breakfast have been tea, coffee and chocolate. These
are discussed at length below.

Breakfast has sometimes been an occasion for hospitality. This is now
confined to the older universities, but was once quite common, especially
during the nineteenth century. Among many others Samuel Rogers, whose
Table Talk was edited and published in 1856, was celebrated for his breakfast
parties, attended by a circle which at one time included Byron. Of a rather
similar character, in that the occasions differ from the ordinary breakfast,
are the *Wedding Breakfast* and the *Hunt Breakfast* (Plate 38), both distinguished
by a menu considerably more substantial than is usual. The menu for the
wedding breakfast is similar to that of luncheon; that for a hunt breakfast
is more an unusually large but normal breakfast.

The second meal to be considered here is Dinner. Though the name is
that now given in many households to the last meal eaten during the day
(except on Sunday), dinner during the later Middle Ages was commonly
eaten before noon. From that point there seems to have been a steady
slipping onward of the hour; in 1900 an average time in England was 7.30
p.m. Many of the stages in this forward movement of the dinner hour are

recorded. In Cromwell's day a common hour seems to have been 1 p.m., though there must have been many who still retained a preference for 10 or 11. Early in the next century Steele records in *The Tatler* for 1712 that during his lifetime the dinner hour had slipped from 12 to 3,* but we cannot help observing that other evidence suggests that 3 p.m. for the early eighteenth century was a very late hour. A story of Pope and Lady Suffolk, referring to 1740, recounts her wish to delay the dinner hour until 4, and his refusal to wait so long.* Together with this we may recall the lines from *The Rape of the Lock*, though they do not name a definite hour.

> 'Meanwhile declining from the noon of day
> The sun obliquely shoots his burning ray;
> The hungry Judges soon the sentence sign,
> And wretches hang that Jurymen may dine.'*

By the middle years of the century, a common hour was 3 p.m. This is born out by Goldsmith's *The Haunch of Venison*.

> 'Tomorrow you take a poor dinner with me;
> No words—I insist on't—precisely at three.'*

The diarist Parson Woodforde tells us several times that his regular dinner hour was 3 p.m.* Boswell is not very illuminating about the dinner hour, which he seldom records, and all we can say is that he seems usually to have risen from the table by 5 p.m. Towards the end of the eighteenth century, however, 4 p.m. was a common hour, and Maria Josepha Holroyd, who has already been quoted, recounts in the same passage that the family's dinner hour was at 4, after which there was Backgammon, then tea at 7, supper at 10; she went to bed at 11.* The same dinner hour, though not for the same reasons, was chosen by Dr. George Fordyce, the great anatomist. In imitation of the lion he took only one meal a day, at 4 p.m.*

In 1811 the diarist Thomas Creevey dined at 6, but that the dinner hour was liable to profound variation then is shown by the fact that in 1822 he dined at 3.45 p.m.* At about the same date, in 1813, Jane Austen's brother's household at Godmersham dined at 4.30.* Mr. Pickwick's Attorney, Perker, tells a story at breakfast on the morning of the trial in which a foreman of Jury, to keep the Jury's deliberations short, puts his watch on the table and announces 'I dine at 3, Gentlemen'—but high society was already dining at a later hour. By the middle of the century the time seems to have varied between 5.30 and 6.30 and while 7.30 is a fair average for 1900, it seems likely that there were great numbers who dined at a later hour.

It is difficult or impossible to generalize about the food eaten at dinner during this period, since it varies as much in quantity as it does in variety. Something, however, must be included on the subject of Carving. It has been suggested already that the medieval Carver's position was largely ceremonial, and that as it began to become active in the fifteenth century it became less popular. Assistants to the Carver appear in the early Ordinances, and although as late as the seventeenth century Henrietta Maria's household included Carvers, the position had already begun to pass away. We hear of this first in Ben Jonson's play, *The Devil is an Ass* II. viii (acted in 1614). This evidence, like that of the seventeenth century pictures shown, dates from before the Restoration and therefore belongs in strict chronology to the medieval section of this book; but like the seventeenth century pictures, it shows the beginning of the new rather than a continuation of the old, and is therefore included at this point. Jonson has here a passage where Dick Robinson, a boy actor, is described as able to perform various feminine duties including Carving.

> '. . . and now, he Sir brought *Dick Robinson*,
> Dresd like a Lawyer's wife amongst 'hem all;
> (I lent him cloathes) but, to see him behave it
> And lay the law; and carve; and drink unto him . . .'

During the seventeenth century the Carver as a specially appointed officer is very seldom heard of, and the task of carving which was at first for

Steele, *The Tatler*, No. 263.

Quoted by Arnold Palmer, *Movable Feasts* (London, 1952), p. 8.

Pope, *The Rape of the Lock*, canto III, lines 19-22.

Goldsmith, *The Haunch of Venison* (published in 1774 but said to have been written in 1771) stanza 4, lines 3 to 4.

The Diary of a Country Parson, by James Woodforde. July 18, 1768; October 25, 1781. The latter reference states Woodforde's rule.

Arnold Palmer, *op. cit.*, p. 17.

Edith Sitwell, *The English Eccentrics* (New York, 1957), p. 214.

Herbert Maxwell (ed.) *The Creevey Papers* (London, 1904). Letter to Mrs. Creevey 21st January, 1811, and letter to Miss Ord 12th February, 1822.

Letter to Cassandra Austen, November 6th, 1813, from Godmersham, Kent.

Plate 43. Covered cup, silver-gilt. Ht. 13⅝". London, 1744, by George Wickes. Toronto, Lee of Fareham Collection.

host and hostess, seems to have been spread much more generally, among the host, the hostess and all the guests. In the eighteenth century this was still the case; thus Lord Chesterfield writes in a letter to his son 'Have you learned to carve? for it is ridiculous not to carve well', and more formally 'Since I am upon little things, I must mention another, which, though little enough in itself, yet, as it occurs at least once in every day, deserves some attention: I mean carving. Do you use yourself to carve *adroitly* and genteely, without hacking half an hour across a bone, without bespattering the company with the sauce, and without overturning the glasses into your neighbours' pockets?'*

It is clear from many eighteenth century sources that the guest was frequently called on to carve. Boswell gives an illustration of this in the *Life*:

'The cheering sound of "Dinner is upon the table" dissolved his reverie, and we *all* sat down without any symptom of ill humour. There were present, beside Mr. Wilkes, and Mr. Arthur Lee, who was an old companion of mine when we studied physick at Edinburgh, Mr. (now Sir John) Miller, Dr. Lettsom, and Mr. Slater, the druggist. Mr. Wilkes placed himself next to Dr. Johnson, and behaved to him with so much attention and politeness, that he gained upon him insensibly. No man eat more heartily than Johnson, or loved better what was nice and delicate. Mr. Wilkes was very assiduous in helping him to some fine veal. "Pray give me leave, Sir;—It is better here—A little of the brown—Some fat, Sir—A little of the stuffing—Some gravy—Let me have the pleasure of giving you some butter—Allow me to recommend a squeeze of this orange; or the lemon, perhaps, may have more zest."—"Sir, Sir, I am obliged to you, Sir," cried Johnson, bowing and turning his head to him with a look for some time of "surly virtue", but, in a short while, of complacency.'*

We cannot say exactly how long this arrangement of various carvers lasted, but Alexis Soyer's *The Gastronomic Regenerator*, 1848, has a passage which bears on it.

'Very few persons are perfect in this useful art, [sc. carving] which requires not only grace, but a great deal of skill. Others become very nervous; many complain of the knife, which has not the least objection to be found fault with; or else they say, this capon, pheasant, or poularde is not young, and

Alexis Soyer, The Gastronomic Regenerator, 1848, p. xiv.

Charles Cooper, The English Table in History and Literature (London, n.d.), p. 22.

consequently not of the best quality. You may sometimes be right, but it certainly often happens that the greatest gourmet is the worst carver, and complains sadly during that very long process, saying to himself, "I am last to be served; my dinner will be cold."*

In preparation for carving, there was in the 1840's an establishment in Soho in which ladies were given instructions in the art,* the learner being required to provide the joint used. Mrs. Beeton makes no specific reference to carving, but she does include notes and in many cases a plan of the animal in question and of the joints of meat that came from it. Some later books refer to the carving being done by the Butler at a sidetable, but they are a small minority.

The Victorians seem often to have preferred formality to informality, and there was at least a return to one person to do the carving— the host or a guest specially asked to do it. After this custom was established, the subject is not mentioned again.

Only a very few words are necessary here about Supper. The first definition in the OED is 'the last meal in the day', but here we must read 'meal' as meaning 'formal meal', to give the definition any meaning. We have seen above that the Eltham Ordinances of 1526 give the dinner hour as 11 a.m. and the supper hour as 6 p.m. The 'Solemn Supper' at which the ghost of Banquo appeared to Macbeth (Macbeth III. iv) was at 7 p.m. As the dinner hour was pushed steadily forward, the supper hour followed suit, keeping something close to the original distance of five or six hours. By about 1800, when dinner was eaten between 5 and 6 p.m., the supper hour began to tangle with bed time. The author of A New System of Domestic Cookery, 1809, which is dealt with more fully below, remarks that 'Hot suppers are not much in use where people dine very late'.* Old Mr. Woodhouse, in Jane Austen's Emma, 'liked to see the cloth laid [for supper] because it had been the fashion of his youth'*—which must be dated before 1750 when dinner was eaten very much earlier—and there must have been many others like him. Nothing, however, could hold back the onward movement of the dinner hour, and as the nineteenth century advances supper is less and less often mentioned. By the last quarter of the century it had plainly ceased to be a regularly eaten meal.

As the pressure of daily work combined with other forces to push the breakfast hour back and the dinner hour forward, and thus lengthen the gap

A New System of Domestic Cookery, 1809, p. 322.

Jane Austen, Emma, 1816, chapter III.

Plate 47b. Glass pedestal bowl, 9⅜", 1820-1840, English or Irish. Toronto, Royal Ontario Museum.

between them to perhaps ten or eleven hours, other meals had to be invented to fill in the time. The first of these is lunch, which began during the later Middle Ages as a quite irregular light meal often eaten out-of-doors, and known as Nunchin, defined in Johnson's *Dictionary* of 1755 as a 'piece of victuals eaten between meals'. The two alternative present forms of the word, Lunch and Luncheon, both date from the last years of the seventeenth century. Luncheon is defined by Johnson as 'as much food as one's hand can hold'. Lunch long retained the incidental character of its earlier days, and not until far into the nineteenth century was it recognized as a regular feature of daily life. It interfered with the day's work, and when admitted at all it was in many cases kept to a minimum. It is believed that so many of our nineteenth century ancestors declined to eat lunch at all that they provoked an increase in the size of dinner to make up for it.

The time for lunch has not commonly been later than 1.30 p.m., and 1 p.m. is a more popular hour. As the hour of dinner moved ever further forward, however, it still left a long and lengthening gap between it and lunch, and it was found desirable to fill this gap in some way. Many sets of memoirs written in the middle of the last century bear out the theory that tea-drinking in the afternoon gradually became a quite general custom as soon as the dinner hour was pushed far enough forward to justify it, and it seems that what began as merely a 'cup of tea' became another meal.

Unconvincing claims to the 'invention' of afternoon tea as a separate meal have been made, but since the drinking of tea after the large midday meal had already replaced beer and wine drinking as an established social custom, it seems hardly necessary to search for an 'inventor'.

Whatever may be the truth of this, Afternoon Tea as a formal meal seems to date only from the latter part of the nineteenth century. It varied greatly in scope, and the 1880 editor of Mrs. Beeton distinguishes two types.

'There is Tea and Tea, the substantial family repast in the house of the early diner, and the afternoon cosy, chatty affairs that the late diners have instituted. Both are eminently feminine; both should be as agreeable and social as possible. The family tea-meal is very like that of breakfast, only that more cakes and knickknackery in the way of sweet eatables are provided. A "High Tea" is where meat takes a prominent part and signifies really, what it is, a tea-dinner. A white cloth is used, and two trays, one for tea, and one for coffee prepared, as at breakfast. Hot buttered cakes, plain and sweet, are chiefly used at tea. And there is the mere cup of tea that the lady or ladies of the house take after their afternoon drive as a kind of reviver before dressing for dinner. The afternoon tea signifies little more than tea and bread-and-butter, and a few elegant trifles in the way of cake and fruit. This meal is simply to enable a few friends to meet and talk comfortably and quietly, and, therefore, there is never a large party asked. There are proper services for these afternoon teas, exceedingly pretty and good.
'When, however, there is really a veritable tea-party, such as our grandmothers delighted to give—and these are far from unfashionable—the repast differs little from the family one just mentioned; only that there would be extra provision made and, probably, more attention bestowed upon it.'*

In passing we may note that although tea is the most recent meal to be introduced, it has, probably because of its feminine origin, the distinction of a special costume not worn at any other time. This was the 'tea gown', perhaps first mentioned in a woman's magazine in 1877* and which remained in fashion until after the end of our period.

Although Afternoon Tea dates only from the nineteenth century, the introduction of tea to Europe dates from the first part of the seventeenth. It was known in Holland in 1637, in England in 1659. It seems to have grown slowly in popularity—Pepys only mentions tea on the first occasion he drank it '. . . I sent for a cup of Tee, a China drink'*—and to have been long considered as a purely or largely medicinal drink. It was not until after 1707 that the price was reduced, and imports rose to astonishing heights— five million pounds in 1766 and eight million two years later. These figures were due partly to a change made in the Licensing Law in 1751, which caused a steep increase in the price of gin.

Whereas tea had to be brought from China and the Far East—the import of it from India is a result of the ending of the East India Company's monopoly in 1833 and dates only from 1839—coffee and chocolate both came from rather nearer home, coffee from the Near East and chocolate from the West Indies. Coffee is referred to in Evelyn's *Diary* as having been drunk by a Greek, Nathaniel Conopios, when Evelyn was at Christ Church, Oxford in the 1630's and Coffee Houses in London date from 1652 or soon after. It seems to reach its height with Johnson's 'Frank, go and get coffee and let us breakfast in splendour',* but a different impression is given in the letters of C. P. Moritz,

'I would always advise those who wish to drink coffee in England, to mention beforehand how many cups are to be made with half an ounce; or else the people will probably bring them a prodigious quantity of brown water; which (notwithstanding all my admonitions) I have not yet been able wholly to avoid.'*

Mrs. Beeton, *Book of Household Management*, 1880 ed., p. 1242.

C. Willet Cunnington, *English Women's Clothing of the Nineteenth Century* (London, 1937), p. 283.

Diary, 26th September, 1660.

Boswell, *Life*, 4th October, 1779.

C. P. Moritz, *Travels in England in 1782*. Letter of 5th June.

Boswell, *Life*, 16th April, 1779.
Pickwick Papers, Chapter XLIV

Chocolate, though said in Parkinson's *Theatrum Botanicum*, 1640, to be considered by the Europeans in the West Indies as 'wash for hogs' seems to have grown quickly in popularity and was for long a serious rival to coffee as a breakfast drink. Coffee pots and chocolate pots of both silver and other materials survive in large numbers from eighteenth century England, when the two drinks seem to have been equally popular. Only since then has coffee almost entirely supplanted chocolate, in England and elsewhere. Chocolate is mentioned in Brillat-Savarin, *La Physiologie du Goût*, but he nowhere suggests that it was at the time a really popular drink.

Tea, coffee and chocolate, as concomitants to alcoholic drinks, have had a strongly civilizing effect on English society, and must also have played a part in altering the balance between the two sexes in the home. The man is responsible for wine at a meal when it is served. The woman fills or refills tea, coffee or chocolate cups. When one of these latter drinks is served in the drawing room after dinner it is the woman who dispenses it.

The food eaten at afternoon tea seems to have varied just as much as we might expect. At one end of the scale there is the 'cup of tea' already referred to as being consumed after the afternoon drive. Next we may mention the cucumber sandwiches which were eaten by Algernon in Oscar Wilde's *The Importance of being Earnest*. More substantial are crumpets, also referred to in that play, which are the subject of a story Dickens copied from Boswell,* putting the story into the mouth of Sam Weller,* substituting crumpets for muffins, and making it a story of a man 'who killed himself on principle'.

' "Wot have you been a eatin' on?" says the doctor. "Roast weal," says the patient. "Wot's the last thing you dewoured?" says the doctor. "Crumpets," says the patient. "That's it!" says the doctor. "I'll send you a box of pills directly, and don't you never take no more of 'em," he says. "No more o' wot?" says the patient—"Pills?" "No; crumpets," says the doctor. "Wy?" says the patient, starting up in bed; "I've eat four crumpets, ev'ry night for fifteen year, on principle." "Well, then, you'd better leave 'em off, on principle," says the doctor. "Crumpets is wholesome, sir," says the patient. "Crumpets is *not* wholesome, sir," says the doctor, wery fierce. "But they're so cheap," says the patient, comin' down a little, "and so wery fillin' at the price." "They'd be dear to you, at any price; dear if you wos paid to eat 'em," says the doctor. "Four crumpets a night," he says, "vill do your business in six months!" The patient looks him full in the face, and turns it over in his mind for a long time, and at last he says, "Are you sure o' that 'ere, sir?" "I'll stake my professional reputation on it," says the doctor. "How many crumpets, at a sittin', do you think 'ud kill me off at once?" says the patient. "I don't know," says the doctor. "Do you think half a crown's wurth 'ud do it?" says the patient. "I think it might," says the doctor. "Three shillins' wurth 'ud be sure to do it, I s'pose?" says the patient. "Certainly," says the doctor. "Wery good," says the patient; "good night." Next mornin' he gets up, has a fire lit, orders in three shillins' wurth o' crumpets, toasts 'em all, eats 'em all, and blows his brains out.'

At the other extreme there is the menu envisaged by Mrs. Humphry in 1902.

Thé, Café, Pain et Beurre.

Sandwich au Jambon

Sandwich de Langue de Boeuf.

Sandwich d'Anchois.   Sandwich de Foie Gras.

Sandwich d'Oeufs et Cresson.

Bonnes Bouchées aux Huitres.

Côtelettes de Volaille.

Gâteau Savoy   Sponge Rusks   Gâteau Madère.

Gâteau Genoa   Gâteau à la Victoria.

Coeur d'Amandes   Macaroons.

Pâtisserie Française.

Gelée au Marasquin   Gelée aux Fruits.

Gelée à la Russe   Gelée au Vin.

Petits Fours.

Crème à l'Ananas   Crème au Chocolat.

Glace Fraise à la Crème   Citronade.

Soda Water, Aerated and Home-made Lemonade.

Claret Cup.*

Mrs. Humphry, *Etiquette for Every Day*, 1902, p. 64.

As a menu for afternoon tea this vast selection of food is all the indication we need of the Edwardian appetite. Considering that luncheon was eaten not very long before it, and dinner followed moderately soon after it, it seems hardly credible to us today that such a meal could even have been considered, but though the cup of tea occupies a very small space on this list, it was the core of the meal throughout.

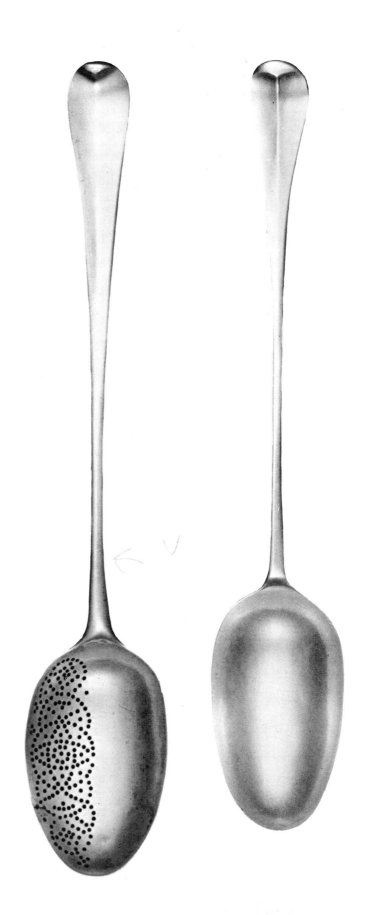

Conduct of meals

No author of any cookery book that appeared much before the middle of the nineteenth century mentions any meals except dinner and supper; even the editions of Mrs. Beeton published before 1880 give only a few lines to breakfast, perhaps half a page to luncheon, and of course do not mention afternoon tea at all. This chapter is therefore concerned almost exclusively with dinner.

We may recall that in the medieval manner of serving meals the guests sat in groups according to rank, each with his own trencher and spoon before him, and perhaps a knife which he took from his pocket. Food was placed in the centre of the table for the whole group on one or more of the large dishes, and each diner took what he wanted and put it on the trencher in front of him. The thumb and finger were normally used for this purpose and for carrying the food to the mouth, but the services of a knife may often have been called on. The spoon was for soup, which was served in a bowl similar to that in Plate 25.

The manner began to change sometime about 1600 into the first stage of

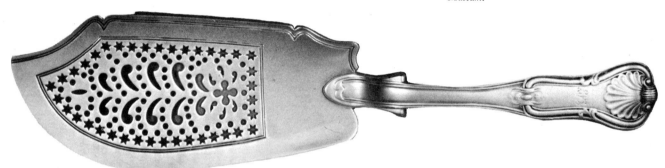

Plate 51. Fish slice, silver. Length 12". London, 1815, by Paul Storr. Toronto, Royal Ontario Museum.

the modern one, seen in the engraving of James I and the Spanish Ambassador (?) at dinner which, as has been said, dates from about 1700 (Plate 32), and in the Houckgeest painting of Charles I (Plate 33). The manner of eating is not clear in either case, but seems to involve the use of knives and forks. The really striking change, however, is that the large medieval dish has now given way to a number of smaller dishes, some shown on the table and some as being held by the many servants. We may suppose that each of the viands listed on the royal menus in the Eltham Ordinances was now contained in a separate dish. Both scenes, however, show two of the distinguishing marks of the Middle Ages. In that of James I all the diners except the Prince of Wales wear hats, and in that of Charles I the King does the same. In both scenes one side of the table is left free for the service.

Many of the dishes in both these seventeenth century versions are scattered over the table, and it seems that this was a first stage in the development. A second seems to occur at about the end of the century. Here the whole or a very large part of the surface of the table was covered by a neat arrangement of dishes. Several of the cookery books give diagrams of this, beginning with Henry Howard's *England's Newest Way*, 1703, and reaching perhaps the highest level in Mrs. Smith's *The Compleat Housewife*, 1727 (Plates 39 and 40). These diagrams show that, in contrast to the medieval lack of arrangement, there had by about 1700 begun the modern progression of soup—fish—meat—sweet dishes, which seems to have followed the Restoration. Most of the diagrams seem to allow no space at the table for the diners, and it has already been suggested that what the diagrams in Mrs. Smith's book really show may be a side table rather than the dining table proper.

A number of the later eighteenth century cookery books include similar plans for the arrangement of the table, but it becomes more usual to give the effect of the engraved plan merely by the arrangement of the type. An example of this is in *A New System of Domestic Cookery*, 1807. This gives Bills of Fare for each month, in the eighteenth century manner, but they are in very general terms and lack details. Following them there are much more detailed suggestions for family dinners (of up to eleven dishes) giving the exact manner in which each dish is to be cooked.

Examples of these more detailed menus are given below. These require an explanation since they include the rather mysterious word in use during much of the first part of the nineteenth century (not used by Mrs. Beeton), Remove. The Remove appears in the *OED* in a quotation from the fourth edition of Johnson's *Dictionary*, 1773, where it is defined as 'a dish to be changed while the rest of the course remains'. It next appears in Parson Woodforde's *Diary* for 1796.* In his description of a dinner are the words '. . . Salmon boiled and Shrimp Sauce, some White Soup, Saddle of Mutton

April 20, 1796.

Plate 52. Dinner Table laid for a Party of Ten, from the 1880 edition of Mrs. Beeton, Book of Household Management.

rosted & Cucumber &c., Lambs Fry, Tongue, Breast of Veal ragoued, rich Pudding the best part of a Rump of Beef stewed immediately after the Salmon was removed'. It seems that the Remove was part of the practice of placing all the dishes for each course on the table. It was a dish that for some reason was removed before the course was over and replaced by another dish, but our quotations end with one from Thackeray dated 1852.

FAMILY DINNERS

FIVE DISHES

Knuckle of Veal stewed with Rice

Apple Sauce   Bread and Butter   Potatoes

Pudding

Loin of Pork roasted

ELEVAN AND ELEVAN, AND TWO REMOVES

(FIRST COURSE)

Salmon

(*Remove — Brisket of Beef stewed, and high Sauce*)

Cauliflower

Fry   Shrimp Sauce   Pigeon Pie

Stewed   Giblet Soup   Stewed Peas
Cucumbers   and Lettuce

Potatoes

Cutlet   Anchovy Sauce   Veal Olives
Maintenon   braised

Soles fried

(*Remove — Quarter of Lamb roasted*)

(SECOND COURSE)

Young Peas

Coffee Cream   Ramakins

Lobster

Raspberry   Orange
Tart   Trout

Trifle

Grated Beef

Omelet   Roughed Jelly

Ducks

A New System of Domestic Cookery has a further interest for us. By the closing years of the eighteenth century social changes, perhaps spurred on by events in France, had begun to alter many of the earlier table customs, including that of serving meals. These alterations seem to have been of two kinds. The first is referred to by the author in the words

'In some houses one dish at a time is sent up with the vegetables and sauces proper to it; and this, in succession, hot and hot [sic.]. In others, a course of Soups and Fish; then Meats and boiled Fowls, Turkey, etc. Made Dishes and Game follow; and lastly, Sweet Dishes: but these are not the common modes.'

The second is the introduction of dinner *à la Russe*. This seems also to have been a reaction to the eighteenth century practice of laying all the dishes on the table. It was introduced to Paris in 1810 by the Russian Ambassador, and gradually gained acceptance in both France and England. All the early editions of Mrs. Beeton, however, are extremely doubtful of the practicability of dinner *à la Russe*, the real essence of which in its original form was that all the service, the carving included, was carried out in the kitchen, and which Mrs. Beeton felt involved a much greater amount of cutlery of all kinds than the average household would possess. Nothing remained to be put on the dining table except decorative pieces such as flower vases, the cruets (whatever form they take), sauce boats, implements, glasses and napkin for each place. In this it is quite different from the eighteenth century form of service with everything laid out on the table, which came to be known, to mark the contrast, as dinner *à la Française*.

The early editions contain two pages on Service *à la Russe* directly after the menus for the twelve months.

The later nineteenth century sees a veering of fashion between these two. The successive editors of Mrs. Beeton obviously preferred dinner *à la Française*, though they pay a great deal of attention to dinner *à la Russe*, and include a number of menus for it.* On the other hand, a different view appears in the anonymous *Party-giving on Every Scale*, 1882

'The ostensible improvement in the dinners of today over those of a dozen years ago is that they are served more expeditiously, and that dinner *à la Russe* is universal . . .'

Towards the end of the century there grew up the modern method of serving dinner, in which carving is done in the dining room by the host or an invited guest, on the dinner table or the sideboard, and plates and vegetables are then handed to the diners by a servant. It may be seen as a compromise between dinner *à la Française* and *à la Russe*, though it seems to have in it more of the dinner *à la Française*.

These changes, dating from the early part of the nineteenth century, leave only one set of arrangements for large dinners that we have not yet touched on, those given by Mrs. Beeton. She gives plans and suggested menus for dinners for eighteen (later reduced to sixteen) people (Plate 41). For the majority of these and for the Family Dinners which she suggests, no plans are given. Samples of suggested menus are:

Plate 54. *Cruet stand, silver. Ht.* 8½″. *London, 1760, by John Dalmester. Toronto, Royal Ontario Museum.*

DINNER FOR 12 PERSONS (January)

First Course: Carrot Soup à la Crécy; Oxtail Soup; Turbot and Lobster sauce; fried Smelts with Dutch sauce.

Entrées: Mutton cutlets, with Soubise sauce; Sweetbreads; Oyster Patties; fillets of Rabbits.

Second Course: roast Turkey; stewed Rump of Beef à la Jardinière; boiled Ham, garnished with Brussels Sprouts; boiled Chickens and Celery sauce.

Third Course: roast Hare; Teal; Eggs à la Neige; Vol-au-Vent of Preserved Fruit; 1 Jelly; 1 Cream; Potatoes à la Maître d'Hôtel; grilled Mushrooms; fondue.
Dessert and Ices.

DINNER FOR 10 PERSONS (January)

First Course: Soup à la Reine; Whitings au Gratin; crimped Cod and Oyster sauce.

Entrées: Tendrons de Veau; Curried Fowl and boiled Rice.

*Plate 55. Cruet stands. Left, silver with silver-mounted glass bottles and containers for oil, vinegar, sugar, salt, pepper and mustard. Ht. 9½".
London, 1831, by R. Hennell. Toronto, Royal Ontario Museum. Right, silver with silver-stoppered glass bottles for oil and vinegar and silver casters for salt, pepper and ? sugar. Ht. 10½". London, 1753-4, by Samuel Wells. Toronto, private possession.*

Second Course: Turkey, stuffed with Chestnuts, and Chestnut Sauce; boiled Leg of Mutton, English Fashion, with Caper Sauce and mashed Turnips.

Third Course: Woodcocks or Partridges; Widgeon; Charlotte à la Vanille; Cabinet Pudding; Orange Jelly; Blancmange; Artichoke Bottoms; Fondue.

Dessert and Ices.

DINNER FOR 8 PERSONS (January)

First Course: Mulligatawny Soup; Brill, and Shrimp Sauce; Fried Whitings.

Entrées: Fricasseed Chicken; Pork Cutlets, with Tomato Sauce.

Second Course: Haunch of Mutton; boiled Turkey and Celery sauce; boiled Tongue, garnished with Brussels Sprouts.

Third Course: roast Pheasants; Meringues à la Crème; Compôte of Apples; Orange Jelly; Cheesecakes; Soufflé of Rice; Bondon Cheeses.

Dessert and Ices.

(Four sample menus for six are given, but only one is included here).

DINNER FOR 6 PERSONS (January)

First Course: Julienne Soup; Soles à la Normandie.

Entrées: Sweetbreads, with Sauce Picquante; Mutton Cutlets, with mashed Potatoes.

Second Course: Haunch of Venison; boiled Fowls and Bacon, garnished with Brussels Sprouts.

Third Course: Plum Pudding; Custards in Glasses; Apple Tart; Fondue à la Brillat-Savarin.

Dessert.

PLAIN FAMILY DINNERS FOR JANUARY

Sunday: 1. Boiled Turbot and Oyster Sauce, Potatoes. 2. Roast leg or griskin of Pork, Apple Sauce, Brocoli, Potatoes. 3. Cabinet Pudding, and Damson Tart made with Preserved Damsons.

Monday: 1. The remains of the Turbot warmed in Oyster Sauce, Potatoes. 2. Cold Pork, Stewed Steak. 3.Open Jam Tart, which should have been made with the pieces of paste left from the Damson Tart; baked arrowroot pudding.

Tuesday: 1. Boiled neck of Mutton, Carrots, mashed Turnips, Suet Dumplings, and Caper Sauce; the broth should be served first and a little rice or pearl barley should be boiled with it along with the meat. 2. Rolled Jam Pudding.

Wednesday: 1. Roast Rolled Ribs of Beef, Greens, Potatoes and Horse-radish sauce. 2. Bread-and-butter Pudding, Cheesecakes.

Thursday: 1. Vegetable Soup (the bones from the ribs of Beef should be boiled down with this soup), Cold Beef, mashed Potatoes. 2. Pheasants, Gravy, Bread Sauce. 3. Macaroni.

Friday: 1. Fried Whitings or Soles. 2. Boiled Rabbit and Onion Sauce, minced Beef, Potatoes. 3. Currant Dumplings.

Saturday: 1. Rump-steak pudding or pie, Greens and Potatoes. 2. Baked Custard Pudding and Stewed Apples.

(Two of these Plain Family Dinners are suggested for each month. Only one is included here).

Whatever the manner of serving meals, the first thing placed on the table is the table cloth. The late medieval practice of laying three cloths did not survive, and the three were succeeded, as the 1880 edition of Mrs. Beeton suggests, by either two cloths over the whole of the table, one of which was removed before dessert, or only one cloth, protected at each end by what Mrs. Beeton refers to as either an 'Accident Cloth' or a 'Spatter Cloth'. The Victorians sometimes disposed of the table cloth entirely, though much less often at dinner than at other meals, replacing it with the 'luncheon mat' at each place and thus allowing a large area of the highly polished mahogany table to be seen. This practice had been adopted in the earlier nineteenth century by the Parisian chain of restaurants owned by a Monsieur Duval, but instead of the polished mahogany he provided, for economy's sake, a marble table without any cloth. This, though not English, is mentioned because the example is sadly familiar to us today.

Of the objects placed on the table perhaps the most intentionally decorative was the Cup, which stood in the centre. The medieval Standing Cup was originally and primarily for use: a new type is first seen in the seventeenth century in the vessel now for some reason called a 'porringer' (Plate 42). As time went on this grew enormously in size; by the early nineteenth century it had become a large and impressive piece (Plates 43 and 44). A different approach to the problem of table ornaments appears in the 1880 edition of Mrs. Beeton, which reads at one point 'The centre ornament used to be almost invariably a *plateau* or an *epergne;* but now, an exquisite vase full of flowers is the decoration *par excellence*' (Plate 52). Of the three objects mentioned, the 'exquisite vase of flowers' may be easily dealt with. Vases of flowers have a long history, but neither pictorial nor literary evidence suggests that they were used as dinner table ornaments until about 1800. Evidence of various kinds and of about this date* suggests that by then vases of flowers were quite well known on the dinner table, and it seems that Mrs. Beeton's editor's statement in so far as it suggests that the vase of flowers was anything new in 1880, must be revised.

The *plateau* in modern terms would be called a table-centre, though it was much larger than any of the other pieces bearing the name. It was rectangular in shape, often with rounded ends, on either a low continuous base or short separate legs which raised its surface perhaps two inches above the table, and was normally made in a number of much smaller rectangular

e.g. *A New System of Domestic Cookery*, 1807, p. 323.

These are referred to in Macquoid and Edwards, *Dictionary of English Furniture*, 1st ed. 1927, vol. III, o. 47; 2nd ed. by R. Edwards, 1954, vol. III, p. 35, fig. 1.

pieces.* It was the English version of the French *surtout de table*, and was adapted in England under European, presumably French, influence. Examples of the *plateau* are rare; the European ones are often of mirror glass with a continuous edging made of porcelain, and date from about the middle of the century: English examples were often of wood, japanned or painted with floral designs, or of papier mâché. One, said to have belonged to the

Plate 56. Decanters, the smaller one wheel-engraved with a pen and a rose for George and William Penrose. Hts. 9¾″, 11⅛″. The larger English, 3rd quarter 18th century, the smaller Irish, late 18th century. Toronto, Royal Ontario Museum.

historian Edward Gibbon, is shown in Plate 45. The earliest literary reference given in the *OED* is a letter of George Washington dated 1791; such references stretch thinly through the period from then until 1861. The most detailed mention is that of Dickens in *Dombey and Son;* his reference to the 'frosted Cupids' echoes other descriptions of *plateaux*, which seem to have been of much the same character:

'and the long plateau of precious metal frosted, separating him from Mrs. Dombey, whereon frosted Cupids offered scentless flowers to each of them, was allegorical to see.'*

Charles Dickens, *Dombey and Son* (London, 1848), chapter XXXVI.

The next object mentioned in Mrs. Beeton is the *epergne*, defined in the *OED* as 'Centre-dish or centre ornament for the dinner table, now often in a branched form, each branch supporting a small dish for dessert or the like or a vase for flowers.' In origin it seems at first to have been a stand for pickles, and a bill of fare for 1761 speaks of 'Two Grand *Epergnes* filled with fine pickles'. It seems very soon to have acquired a wider purpose, and in the last quarter of the eighteenth century it was a method economical in space of

placing on the table nuts, sweets or small fruits; an example in silver of 1792-3 by Henry Chawner is illustrated in Plate 46. The earliest literary references belong to the third quarter of the eighteenth century. The *epergne* has no place on any of Mrs. Smith's table plans of 1727, but is referred to later in the century by Horace Walpole in a letter dated March 4, 1763, describing the silver given by George III to Queen Charlotte's brother, the Duke of Mecklenberg-Strelitz. He speaks of 'Dishes, plates without number, an *epergne*, candlesticks, salt cellars, sauce boats and tea and coffee equipages . . .'

Another form of dining table ornament which dates from about the same time but is of a quite different character is the model or miniature garden. This is referred to by Parson Woodforde in 1783, describing an example in the possession of the Bishop of Norwich

'A most beautiful Artificial Garden in the Centre of the Table remained at dinner and afterwards, it was one of the prettiest things I ever saw, about a Yard long, and about 18 Inches wide, in the middle of which was a high round Temple supported on round Pillars, the Pillars were wreathed round with artificial Flowers—on one side was a Shepherdess on the other a Shepherd, several handsome Urns decorated with artificial Flowers, etc. etc.'*

Diary, September 4, 1783.

These miniature gardens must originally have been made by the ladies of a household. Later they were made commercially, and a fashion for them seems to have lasted through most of the first three quarters of the nineteenth century.* We must assume that this form of table ornament was going out of fashion by about 1875, since although there was a competition for a design in the Royal Horticultural Society Exhibition in Birmingham in 1873, Mrs. Beeton's editor makes no mention of it in 1880.

*These decorations are dealt with in Bea Howe, 'Decorating the Victorian Dinner Table', *Country Life*, January 7, 1960, p. 10f.

Between them these seem to be the first indications we have of any purely decorative object being placed on the table—disregarding, that is, the much earlier sugar figures. With the flower vase may be mentioned another feature of the nineteenth century, a vessel on a high stem and foot that was made in a great variety of materials. The earliest examples are of English or Irish glass, dating from the late eighteenth or the early nineteenth century. Contemporary sources describe all of them as 'salad bowls', though it is generally assumed that they served other purposes as well. The shapes of bowl, stem and foot vary much; most of the early ones have deep bowls (often oval in shape), tall stems to place them well above the surface of the table, and feet which in the earliest examples are deep and square, in later ones flat and round (Plate 47). In later years this piece was made in many materials, and many variations of the original shape. It now often had a flat plate instead of the bowl, and a tall thin stem. The 1869 Mrs. Beeton illustrates many of these on pages 832 and 833. It may have been at this time that it acquired the quite inappropriate name of 'tazza' (Italian for cup) which still sticks to it.

After the table cloth and the decorative objects, the implements of eating are to be considered. Knives, forks and spoons were all provided by the host throughout this modern period. The knife has changed little since it acquired a rounded, not pointed end: the chief variation has been in the handle; of the large types, the most notable English example is the 'pistol grip' of the earlier eighteenth century: it may have been popular because it was found much more comfortable to the hand (Plate 48); knife handles were often of carved ivory, painted china or enamelled metal.

In the later seventeenth century there had been a great change in the shapes of both spoon and fork: the bowl of the spoon changed from the earlier fig shape to the egg shape that is used now; the handle from the round type of the Middle Ages to the flat type of today (Plate 49). The fork came very slowly into general use. In the seventeenth century it was sometimes made in a pair with the knife and had a similar decorative handle. Being placed on the table next to the spoon, as it came to be perhaps during

Plate 57. Decanter, glass. Ht. 10¼". English or Irish, late 18th or early 19th century. Toronto, Royal Ontario Museum.

the eighteenth century, it was made in the same design (Plate 49) and, like the spoon, of silver. Its development has been the increase in the number of tines from two to four: examples with three and four tines were both known in the seventeenth century, but only came into general use towards 1800.

The carving knife, fork and steel, have varied little from their late medieval forerunners. The steel was beginning to pass out of use at about the end of our period.

With the carving knife and fork may be mentioned the very large serving spoons which seem to become common in the eighteenth century (Plate 50), the small ladles for sauce which also first appear in this century and the very large ladles for soup and punch which came in almost the same time.

Fish was for a long time eaten with the same knife and fork as other foods, and still sometimes is. The idea that the flavour of fish becomes unpleasant if steel touches it seems to date back to the eighteenth century, and an early example is found in Boswell's *Tour to the Hebrides*:

'The old tutor of Macdonald eat fish with his fingers, alleging that a knife and fork gave it a bad taste. I took the liberty to observe to Mr. Johnson that he [i.e. Dr. Johnson] did so. "Yes," said he; "but it is because I am short-sighted, and afraid of bones; for which reason I'm not fond of eating many kinds of fish, because I must take my fingers." '*

Boswell, *Journal of a Tour to the Hebrides* (Malahide Papers) (Toronto, 1936), p. 165.

There is nothing to suggest anything special in the service of fish until almost 1800. The silver or plated fish knife and fork came into use then, and at the same time the silver or plated fish slice and fork replaced the steel knife and fork when fish was served. The first reference is in *Hints on Etiquette*, 1836, where the relevant section begins

'The application of a knife to fish is likely to destroy the delicacy of its flavour; besides which, fish sauces are often acidulated; acids corrode steel, and draw from it a disagreeable taste'.

The shape of both fish knife and fork have varied little; the early editions of Mrs. Beeton illustrate a special fish fork to accompany the slice, but this is not always preserved. A slice without its fork is illustrated in Plate 51.

The supposed taint of steel on fish is parallelled on fruit, and silver or plated fruit knives and forks also date from the late eighteenth century. The fruit knife seems to have enjoyed a rather longer life than the fish knife, and has kept its narrow shape and pointed end without change.

On the left side of each place it has been usual, for one hundred years at least, to find a small china plate holding a roll or a slice of bread. The rule of etiquette is and has for some time been, that this bread should be broken with the hands and not cut. The diner's napkin is now generally laid flat on or beside this small plate. It has been claimed that the napkin went out of use in the seventeenth and eighteenth centuries, only to return in the nineteenth,* but this seems extremely unlikely. A height of elaboration is reached in the late nineteenth century habit of folding it in many curious and fanciful shapes, to which the 1880 edition of Mrs. Beeton devotes an illustration showing the late Victorian napkin with some of these elaborations.

Cooper, *The History of the English Table*, p. 14.

Containers for salt, pepper and mustard are normally placed towards the centre of the table, as is the Cruet Stand for oil and vinegar if the dinner requires one. Since the Restoration the container for salt has usually been either upright and closed, or a flat open holder similar to the example of 1607-8 shown in Plate 10, but in the eighteenth century it was most often either round or with pointed ends. Early containers for mustard are shrouded in some mystery. It is generally supposed that mustard was eaten dry before it began to be made into a paste; the paste may have appeared about 1700, and a French traveller to England whose experiences were published in an English translation in 1719, describes what seems to be mustard made in the

Plate 58. Decanter, clear and coated glass. Ht. 11½". English, 19th century. Toronto, Royal Ontario Museum.

The French is given in full in Drummond, *The Englishman's Food*, 2nd edition 1957, p. 105.

modern manner and laid on the side of the plate next to the salt.*

However, no containers earlier than 1737 obviously intended for mustard are known. About and shortly after 1700 upright casters were usual, often in sets of three (Plate 53), and as a separate and larger caster was already in use for sugar it seems likely on the face of it—and no satisfactory alternative has even been suggested—casters were intended for salt, pepper and dry mustard: such sets exist today dating from about 1700 until about 1725.

Rather later there grew up a habit, which remained long in use, of making the salt and pepper and mustard holders a part of the cruet set with the oil and vinegar. We first hear of the 'cruet stand' in the early eighteenth century, and its earliest form, by John Dalmester, London, 1760, is shown in Plate 54. This is merely a small stand holding two silver-stoppered glass bottles for oil and vinegar. Another type was in use at the same time, and an example with silver-stoppered glass bottles for oil and vinegar and silver casters for salt, pepper and possibly sugar (the mustard pot having supposedly

Plate 59. *Flagons, silver. Ht. 15½". Edinburgh. 1835, by J. McKay. Toronto, Royal Ontario Museum.*

been separate) by Samuel Wells, London, 1753-4, is shown in Plate 55 (Right). A rather more developed form of stand by Robert Hennell, London, 1831, is also shown in Plate 55 (Left). This has glass containers with silver necks; those that seemed to be for oil, vinegar, salt and pepper have glass stoppers, there are casters for two sorts of sugar, and a mustard pot with silver spoon and lid. The oval stand is rather rounder than the earlier example.

This sort of many-purposed cruet stand continued in intermittent use until the end of our period, and when the 1880 editor of Mrs. Beeton speaks of 'the family cruet stand' it may be to this that she is referring. The nineteenth century seems to see periods of alternating use of the independent salt and pepper holders, mustard pot and cruet stand for oil and vinegar only and of the all-purpose cruet stand. By 1900 the latter was passing finally out of use in private houses. It remains only in some hotels.

Glass is the only material now accepted for drinking vessels for an ever increasing variety of wine and other alcoholic drinks (a notable exception to this rule being beer and ale, for which silver and pewter tankards are often preferred). Since the Restoration, glass has replaced pottery as the material used for this purpose, and we have now to consider briefly its many forms. The first use is as a storage vessel, and the seventeenth century vessels follow very closely the forms and shapes used in pottery. Glass vessels must have been in use at the same time for storing wine, and an example of about 1650* is preserved. It has a roundish body and a straight vertical neck. The types of the second half of the century show small variations in the shape and size of the body, but there are no major new developments. The next type to concern us is the 'decanter-bottle', a vessel with a much larger and rather

Thorpe, *English Glass*, 1935, p. 118.

pear-shaped body, with the same narrow neck above it, after having a narrow raised ring just below the top to hold in place the string that held the cork. The 'taper decanter' appears in the second quarter of the century; it represents the perfection of 'the decanter-bottle' form (Plate 56) and now has a glass stopper. What must have been one of this form is mentioned in a glass-seller's advertisement in the 1720's.

Towards the end of the century a new type with a short neck and a wide barrel-shaped body replaces them (Plate 57), and variations on these forms continued to be made throughout the nineteenth century. One of the variants is shown on Plate 58.

The Measey-Greene drawings are reproduced, *ibid.*, p. 173.

The three-piece wine glass—bowl, stem and foot—is believed to have been a Venetian invention of the sixteenth century. It was soon in use in England, and appears in the drawings connected with John Greene of about 1670.* From roughly 1685 to 1800 five types of stem in wine glasses are significant; the baluster, the plain stem, the air twist, the enamel twist, and the cut stem. Eighteenth century wine glasses tend to be dated by the stem, and the stem in turn to depend largely on this progression of types; in size, wine glasses depend largely on whether they are before or after the Glass Excise Act of 1745-6. Examples of the two types are illustrated in Plates 60 and 61. The bowls of eighteenth century wine glasses vary enormously in type and for every one of the five types of stem that have been listed there are three or four varieties of bowl. In this field, the nineteenth century adds little more than a bewildering variety of bowls, including many that are merely new versions of the eighteenth century type.

The varieties of stem and bowl in wine glasses are another special feature of the later part of this period. Another is the steady increase in the number of wine glasses used by each person at a dinner. Whereas in the earlier part of the period it had been usual to allow only one wine glass for each guest, however many wines were served, in the nineteenth century the number of glasses increases greatly, just as the number and variety of wines drunk increased; so that by late in the period a guest might enter the dining room and find on the table before each place, individual wine glasses for sherry, red or white Bordeaux, red or white Burgundy, Moselle or Hock, Champagne, perhaps one glass for wines drunk with the sweet course such as Tokay, and one glass for the dessert wines of Port and Madeira.

Victoria and Albert Museum Picture Book *Bottle Tickets* (London, 1958) *passim*.

As the varieties of wine increased in the latter part of the eighteenth century, there grew up both the habit of using Wine Labels* on the various decanters, and a Coaster to keep the wine moving easily round the table. A pair of wine containers of a different type, shaped like an ordinary jug with cover and narrow neck and bearing no relation to the decanter, are shown in Plate 59.

As the eighteenth century advanced, glass was put to ever increasing uses at the table. The most significant of these is that curious institution the 'finger bowl' or 'finger glass'. The introduction of the finger bowl or finger glass belongs to the second half of the century; the earliest survivors seem to be of about 1780. One of the first to describe the use of the finger bowl is La Rochefoucauld in 1784.

'[Dinner lasts for four or five hours]. The first two are spent in eating . . . after the sweets you are given water in small bowls of very clear glass in order to rinse out your mouth—a custom which strikes me as extremely unfortunnate. The more fashionable do not rinse out their mouths but that seems to me even worse; for, if you use the water to wash your hands, it becomes dirty and quite disgusting. This ceremony over, the cloth is removed . . .'*

La Rochefoucauld, *Mélanges sur l'Angleterre* (*A Frenchman in England*), 1784, p. 29.

Three years later Dr. Trusler in the book already referred to says in his Directions to Servants:

'Where water-glasses are used after dinner, to wash the fingers; to put on

Plate 60. *Flint glass. Ht.* 8⅞″. *English,* 1690-1700. *Toronto, Royal Ontario Museum.*

those glasses half full of clean water, when the table is cleared, but before the cloth is removed.'*

Dr. Trusler, *Honours of the Table* (London, 1788), p. 9.

Describing Susan Price, Fanny's younger sister, paying her first visit to Mansfield Park, Jane Austen explains that

'she was meditating much upon silver forks, napkins and finger-glasses.'

The terms 'finger bowl' and 'finger glass' became common in the nineteenth century, but customs had already altered in one particular. In *Hints on Etiquette*, 1834, Ἀγωγός says,

'Finger glasses, filled with *warm* water, come on with the dessert. Wet a corner of your napkin, and wipe your mouth, then rinse your fingers; but do not practise the *filthy* custom of gargling your mouth at table, albeit the usage prevails amongst a few, who think, *because* it is a foreign habit, it cannot be disgusting'.*

Ἀγωγός , *Hints on Etiquette*, 1834, p. 23.

Mrs. Beeton also touches on the subject. Her passage in the 1869 edition is:

'At some tables finger glasses are placed at the right hand of each person, nearly half filled with cold spring water, and in winter with tepid water . . . At other tables, a glass or vase is simply handed round, filled with perfumed water, into which each guest dips the corner of his napkin, and when needful, refreshes the lips and the tips of the fingers.'*

Mrs. Beeton, *Book of Household Management*. 1869.

The heyday of the finger glass, however, was short. The early examples are straight sided, but this is replaced during the first quarter of the nineteenth century by a shape where the sides bent outwards for a short distance and then inward again; an English or Irish example is shown in Plate 62. By 1880 it had changed its shape and become much more shallow, and its

Mrs. Beeton, *Book of Household Management*, 1880, p. 1241.

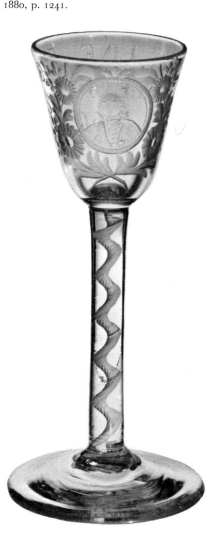

use was becoming less general. The 1880 editor of Mrs. Beeton, although she says in the Directions to Servants,

'Put a finger glass filled within two inches of the brim with cold water in summer and slightly warm in winter, or scented waters, at the right side of the plate.'

adds on the same page

'Finger Glasses are often now omitted entirely.'*

We said in Chapter 5 that three materials—metal, glass and pottery—were typical of the period from 1660 to 1900, and replaced the enormous medieval variety of materials in vessels used on the table. Metal and glass have both been covered, and it now remains to consider pottery, the word being used in its more literal sense of any object made of clay.

The treatment has to be more general than in the cases of either metal or glass, partly because pottery in all its forms—earthenware, stoneware and porcelain—was for long a secondary material, in which objects were only made after they had already appeared in other forms, and partly because a conspiracy of silence seems to cloak pottery until Josiah Wedgwood made it respectable, so that it is impossible to illustrate the points in its history as we were able to do with metal and glass, even when we know that pottery was in use.

The first period of pottery closes with John Dwight's first patent in 1671, and is therefore outside our field here. The second begins in 1671 and lasts until the closing years of the eighteenth century; the third covers the nineteenth. The eighteenth has several features of importance, of which the most noticeable is the steady concentration of the industry, which until then had been rather widespread, in the northern part of Staffordshire. First among these, and in large part the cause of the others, are the technical advances of the first part of the century. These include the new popularity of a white body, resulting first from the use of calcined flints and later of white clay from Dorset and Devon; the habit of moulding clay rather than the old process of throwing, coupled at first with the use of metal moulds, and from the 1740's onwards of Plaster of Paris moulds; and the use of a new form of liquid glazing.

Another was an enormous increase in the volume of the production of all forms of pottery, especially the new soft-paste porcelain which has probably been made in England since 1743, a volume which does little to bear out the apprehensions for the future of the pottery industry noted by Josiah Wedgwood in an early diary. There was a great increase in the amount of all forms of pottery used on the table, which went hand in hand with the steady increase in the number of households in which it was used; the most striking feature of this is the appearance, perhaps in the 1730's, of the 'Service'—a number of vessels serving any one meal, all ornamented with the same design.

Plate 62. *One from a set of twelve finger bowls, glass. Ht. 4". English or Irish, 1820-30. Toronto, private possession.*

Another feature of the eighteenth century is the expression in pottery of what has been called 'The Romance of Distance'. In the early part of the century it was distance in space, expressed first above all in Chinese art and in the Europeanized version, chinoiserie, seen on eighteenth century English delft. Later it was the romance of distance in time, expressed in the whole of the Neoclassical Revival, and in this context in the work of Josiah Wedgwood and his followers.

The period from the 1780's until almost 1830 sees the decline of Neoclassicism; it is important as the time of the popularity of lustre ware. There are many claimants to the discovery, the most convincing story being that it was John Hancock of Etruria*, who made the discovery in Staffordshire in the 1780's. This is a red-bodied ware, the surface being covered in whole or in part by the application of metallic oxides, which give an imitation of the general effect—it could not be closer than that—of gold and silver. It was more popular on the tea table than the dinner table, and it has many and varied uses. Its popularity lasted until the 1850's.

The remainder of the century is occupied by the popularity of two wares, both of which show the effect of the interest in experimentation before and shortly after 1800, and of the addition of large quantities of bone ash to the

* G. W. Rhead and F. A. Rhead, *Staffordshire Pots and Potters*, London 1906, p. 271, 272.

body of English porcelain, and so of English china generally. The first is ironstone, patented by Charles James Mason in 1813, although probably widely known at the time. Ironstone has a rather dark and coarse grey body, the surface being covered with a white glaze and ornamented often by distantly chinoiserie patterns in bright colours. The body is often very thick, supposedly so as to allow a certain measure of careless handling. The second of these wares, one that appears also very early in the nineteenth century, is what came at the end of the century to be called 'bone china'. The addition of bone ash allows the ware to be markedly thin, strong, and white in colour, all three characteristics being a contrast to ironstone. It represents the perfection of the porcellanous white ware, the descendant of the 'china', of which English sources begin to speak in the sixteenth century, some, such as Shakespeare in *Measure for Measure* II. i, in the most slighting manner. It attained a new popularity as the eighteenth century advanced.

These two wares, ironstone and bone china, account between them for most of the pottery produced in the later nineteenth century. Their importance in a wider field is that they came into such great popularity at almost the same time as the dichotomy of the nineteenth century from which we still suffer today, between hand-made or 'studio' pottery on one side and machine-made industrial pottery on the other.

The fear of poison, touched on above as one of the characteristics of the later Middle Ages, hardly survived the Restoration. The Caddinet, containing the knife, spoon and napkin, and a small salt container, is referred to in the records of the Coronation Feast of James II 'The Officers of the Pantry . . . brought up the Salt of State and Caddinet'.* It seems to have passed out of use soon afterwards. There are two surviving examples, one hallmarked 1683-4, the other 1688-9, though they both bear the arms of William and Mary (Plate 63); they are the latest piece of relevant evidence.

With this last relic of the late medieval fear of poison we reach the end of the Arrangement of the Table. In the matter of Conduct at Dinner we see after 1660 a steady loosening of the earlier formality, which reaches its climax in the later eighteenth century writers and in the story of the meeting of Johnson and Wilkes, taken from Boswell's *Life* and quoted above. The nineteenth century shows the two mixed but common phenomena of a return to late medieval formalism on one side, the beginnings of the modern complete lack of all formality on the other.

J. Ogilby, *King's Coronation*, 1685, p. 15.

Plate 63. Caddinet, silver-gilt. 14¾″ x 12″. One of a pair hallmarked respectively 1683-4 and 1688-9; the latter by Antony Nelme. On loan to the Victoria and Albert Museum from the Earl of Lonsdale.

Epilogue

Habits of eating and drinking are an expression of the society in which they arise, and undergo radical changes only when it does. We have observed two such sets of habits in England during the period for which there is any continuous evidence, the medieval, practised from an unknown beginning until a watershed of change was reached between about 1600 and 1660, and the modern, current from then until the end of the period in 1900. The medieval began to change into the modern about or shortly before 1600, under the influence first of Italy and then of France. The medieval practice of serving all the food on large uncovered dishes gave way to the modern habit of serving each type of food in a separate covered container. The knife became an object provided by the host instead of carried by the guest and its blade became broader, and round instead of pointed at the end; the fig-shaped bowl and round stem of the medieval spoon gave way to the larger egg-shaped bowl and flat stem of the modern type; the fork came into regular use.

About 1900 another radical change of this kind began, brought about not by influences from abroad but by social changes at home. English society, however, is conservative and traditional in the extreme, and the change has been very slow to appear, although its roots are the same as those of the legislative changes of about 1910. The silver, glass and pottery typical of the period before 1900 have begun to give way to bakelite, plastic and metal foil. The change in the manner of serving meals seen in the picture of James I at dinner may be parallelled by such new developments as that of the Television Dinner, already cooked and requiring only to be warmed, on a special metal foil plate which can be thrown away after the meal, and of the Television Table for use with it. This seems to be one form, possibly only the first sign we can recognize, of a more far-reaching change. Until the present day, dinner has always been regarded as something to be enjoyed for its own sake. These changes suggest that it is now becoming merely an accompaniment to something else considered to be of more importance.

If this really is a trend, it has hardly begun to appear yet, and is not likely to do so until the change of which it is a reflection is much further advanced. In the circumstances it has seemed best to halt this survey at 1900.

Appendices

Appendix I. Dr. Trusler, and the Books of Etiquette

Table manners form a subject with which surprisingly few writers have dealt. The first to do so are of course the writers of what we have called the books of instruction, belonging to the fifteenth and early sixteenth centuries; these have been considered earlier. Following them there seems to be a gap, which apart from a few items such as Richard West's *The Book of Demeanour*, 1619, extends until the very late eighteenth century. Shortly before 1800 many books of this kind were written by a Dr. Trusler. Trusler was a graduate of Emmanuel College, Cambridge, and an ordained clergyman. His many books deal with a variety of subjects, but what concerns us most here is the number he wrote on the topic of manners and behaviour. Some of these are, and others are said in the title to be 'for the use of young people', such as *The/Honours of the Table,/or/Rules for behaviour during meals;/with the/Whole Art of Carving,/. . . for the Use of Young People.* This book appeared in 1788, with a list of the author's other works and the words 'Those who would give their Children a polished education, should not only put into their hands . . . but the following books, by Dr. Trusler.'

This book is important because it reveals to us a number of details of the eighteenth century manner of serving meals, and lets us see how that manner had changed by 1900. Thus he tells us that it was the custom for all the ladies to precede the hostess into the dining room, followed by all the gentlemen preceding the host, but that the modern custom of a gentleman escorting each lady was just coming into fashion. The difficulties caused by the earlier rule were, of course, settled by the accepted Degrees of Precedence mentioned in Chapter 4. When these fell out of use, but the earlier customs described by Dr. Trusler remained, a number of difficulties arose. One of them has been immortalized by Jane Austen (*Persuasion*, Chapter 6) in the person of Anne Eliot's younger sister Mary, of whom one of the other characters says, 'Nobody doubts her right to have precedence of Mamma, but it would be more becoming of her not to be always insisting on it.' Dr. Trusler's passage reads:

'When dinner is announced, the mistress of the house requests the lady first in rank, in company, to show the way to the rest, and walk first into the room where the table is served; she then asks the second in precedence to follow, and after all the ladies are passed, she brings up the rear herself. The master of the house does the same with the gentlemen. Among persons of real distinction, this marshalling of the company is unnecessary; every woman and every man present knows his rank and precedence, and takes the lead, without any direction from the mistress or the master.

'When they enter the dining-room, each takes his place in the same order; the mistress of the table sits at the upper end, those of superior rank next her, right and left; those next in rank following, then the gentlemen, and the master at the lower end; and nothing is considered as a greater mark of ill-breeding, than for a person to interrupt this order, or seat himself higher than he ought. Custom, however, has lately introduced a new mode of seating: A gentleman and a lady sitting alternately round the table, and this for the better convenience of a lady being attended to, and served by the gentleman next her. But notwithstanding this promiscuous seating, the ladies, whether above or below, are to be served in order, according to their rank or age, and after them, the gentlemen in the same manner'.*

Trusler, The Honours of the Table, 1788, p. 3.

In the same way the author explains how the modern custom of the ladies leaving the dining room grew up, in that they first remained until two or three glasses of wine had been drunk, and then moved.

'. . . it is the part of the mistress or master to ask those friends who seem to have dined, whether they would please to have more. As it is unseemly in ladies to call for wine, the gentlemen present should ask them in turn, whether it be agreeable to drink a glass of wine. ("Madam, or &c. will you do me the honour to drink a glass of wine with me?") and what kind of the wine present they prefer, and call for two glasses of such wine accordingly. Each then waits till the other is served, when they bow to each other and drink.

'Habit having made a pint of wine after dinner almost necessary to a man who eats freely, which is not the case with women, and as their sitting and drinking with the men, would be unseemly; it is customary, after the cloth and dessert are removed and two or three glasses of wine are gone round, for the ladies to retire and leave the men to themselves . . .'*

Trusler, The Honours of the Table, 1788, p. 6.

In one way Dr. Trusler appears as a would-be instructor of the young; in another he shows some of the characteristics of the following century, and in fact appears as a bridge between one style of book and another. It was not long after him that the writing of books for the young was superseded by books written for an educational purpose, as their predecessors were, but one of quite different character—the Book of Etiquette. A great many of these appeared from about 1820 onwards, written by real or *soi-disant* members of the aristocracy. To the middle of the twentieth century these books have a rather repulsive fascination; they were written, often in an unpleasantly condescending tone, for members of the newly rich middle classes to read. The latest to interest us here—that published nearest to 1900—is Mrs. Humphry, *Etiquette for Everyday*, London, 1902, but the type continues.

Appendix II. English Cookery Books since 1660.

Among the cookery books popular about the time of the Restoration was the anonymous *The Queen's Closet Opened. Incomparable Secrets in Physick, Chirurgery, Preserving, Candying and Cookery*, 1655. This is one of the cookery books that takes in its view all the female household accomplishments. The type continued into the nineteenth century, and Mrs. Beeton's *Book of Household Management* is perhaps the last. A common later type, dealing with cookery only, appears first in the year of the Restoration in Robert May, *The Accomplisht Cook . . .*, 1660. Robert May's title is interesting partly because he claims that the book includes directions for making the most *Poinant Sauces*, partly because it includes the kind of self-advertisement which is perhaps the inevitable result of these books being written by professional cooks. Thus the title continues *Approved by the Fifty Years Experience and Industry of Robert May in his Attendance on several Persons of Honour.* This perhaps reaches its highest point in Henry Howard's *England's Newest Way in all sorts of Cookery, Pastry and of Pickles that are fit to be used,* 1703, which includes on the title page the list of the noblemen to whom Howard had been cook, starting with the Duke of Ormond.

Henry Howard strikes a new note, partly because his book extends its scope to include the *best receipts for making cakes, Mackroons, biskets, gingerbread, French-bread, etc.,* and partly because of the distantly nationalist note of the title, if that note is to be regarded seriously. For the period about 1700, however, this is a conservative, not a progressive element. In 1656 Will Rabisha's *The Whole Body of Cookery* had claimed on the title page to include receipts *According to the Best Traditions of the English, French, Italian, Dutch, etc.* In 1665 there had been published anonymously *The Compleat Cook. Expressly describing the most ready Ways, whether Italian, Spanish, or French. For . . . the Ordering of Sauces.* This rather international note is not heard again; in the eighteenth century the domination of French cookery had already begun, and in the period that concerns us no other foreign cookery is heard of again.

The eighteenth century sees an enormous enlargement of the scope of cookery books. This appears first in the anonymous *A Collection of above Three Hundred Receipts in Cookery . . . ,* 1719, and later in Mrs. Smith's *The Compleat Housewife: or Accomplish'd Gentlewoman's Companion,* 1727, the earlier editions of which include more than three hundred, the later more than seven hundred recipes. The title page makes it clear that this is a household book, not a collection of recipes, and there is a large section devoted to various cures, including what seems to have been the most famous eighteenth century example, Dr. Meade's cure for the bite of a mad dog. The recipes are divided according to subject, though they are not yet arranged alphabetically. That for cooking a swan is very reminiscent of the Middle Ages, and is given here to show one type:

'*To pot a Swan.* Bone and skin your swan, and beat the flesh in a mortar, taking out the strings as you beat it; then take some clear fat bacon and beat with the swan, and when it is of a light flesh-colour there is bacon enough in it; when it is beaten till it is like dough, it is enough; then season it with pepper, salt, cloves, mace and nutmeg, all beaten fine, mix it well with your flesh, and give it a beat or two all together; then put it in an earthenware pot, with a little claret and fair water, and at the top two pounds of fresh butter spread over it; cover it with coarse paste, and bake it with bread; then turn it out into a dish; squeeze it gently to get out the moisture; then put it in a pot fit for it; and when it is cold cover it with clarified butter, and next day paper it up; in this manner you may do goose, duck, or beef, or hare's flesh.'*

Mrs. Smith, *The Compleat Housewife* (London, 1727), p. 72.

Her mention of A Fasting Day also recalls the earlier books. Among the many indications of a much more modern date are her inclusion of large sections on both puddings and pastry, both of which became much more popular than before as the result of a steep fall in the price of sugar, beginning at the end of the seventeenth century. To Mrs. Smith the difference between a pye and a tart is absolute, since there is a different kind of pastry in each; among the puddings there are recipes for steamed, bread, and rice puddings, pancakes and even custard. There are pages on cakes, including, as some will note with distaste, a number of recipes for seed cake.

'*A good Seed-Cake.* Take five pounds of fine flour well dried, and four pounds of single-refined sugar beaten and sifted; mix the sugar and flour together, and sift them through a hair-sieve; then wash four pounds of butter in rose or orange-flower-water; you must work the butter with your hand till it is like cream, beat twenty eggs, half the whites, and put to them six spoonfuls of sack: then put in your flour, a little at a time; you must not begin mixing it till the oven is almost hot; you must let it lie a little while before you put the cake into the hoop; when you are ready to put it into the oven, put into it eight ounces of candied orange-peel sliced, as much citron, and a pound and half of carraw-comfits; mix all well together, and put it in the hoop, which must be prepared at bottom, and butter'd; the oven must be quick; it will take two or three hours baking; you may ice it if you please.'*

Mushrooms and tripe are both mentioned in various recipes,* and oysters are seen now to have acquired great importance. Oyster Liquor appears very frequently, and an oyster pie is listed.* Later there is a series of recipes for cheese;* cream cheese, cheddar cheese and Newmarket cheese are all mentioned.

Mrs. Smith sets an example that many later writers follow in giving sample menus, of which the following is one:

'A Bill of Fare for every Season of the Year.
For January. First Course.
Collar of Brawn, Bisque of Fish, Soop with Vermicelly, Orange Pudding with Patties, Chine and Turkey, Lamb Pasty, Roasted Pullets with Eggs, Oyster Pye, Roasted Lamb in Joints, Grand Sallad with Pickles.
Second Course.
Wild-Fowl of all Sorts, Chine of Salmon boiled with Smelts, Fruit of all Sorts, Jole of Sturgeon, Collared Pig, Dried Tongues, with salt Sallads, Marinated Fish.
Another First Course.
Soop à-la-royal, Carp Blovon, Tench stewed, with pitch-cocked Eels, Rump of Beef à-la-braise, Turkeys à-la-daube, Wild Ducks comporte, Fricando of Veal, with Veal Olives.
Another Second Course.
Woodcocks, Pheasants, Salmigondin, Partridge Poults, Bisque of Lambe, Oyster Loaves, Cutlets, Turkeys Livers forced, Pippins stewed.'*

This book unlike its medieval predecessors, was written for the beginner, not the expert, and in line with this Mrs. Smith gives various directions of a kind suitable for a beginner. There is a section on the purchase of meat, and she includes elaborate directions for cooking various joints. The influence of France is acknowledged at the outset, in the words

'What you will find in the following Sheets, are Directions generally for dressing after the best, most natural and wholesome Manner, such Provisions as are the Product of our own Country; and in such a Manner as is most agreeable to English Palates; saving, that I have so far temporized, as since we have, to our Disgrace, so fondly admired the French Tongue, French Modes, and also French Messes, to present you now and then with such Receipts of the French Cookery as I think may not be disagreeable to English Palates.'*

French terms appear on many occasions all through the book. A mark of the eighteenth century is that sauce is given recipes of its own. This is a thing which English cookery books from the earliest date onwards occasionally do, though the attention actually given to the sauce, rather than the meat, is not always very great, and it is not even always clear what is the meaning of the recipe.* Other marks of the same kind are that Seville and Bermuda oranges

Mrs. Smith, *The Compleat Housewife* (London, 1727), pp. 170f.

Ibid., pp. 51, 44, e.g.

Ibid., p. 148.

Ibid., p. 99f.

Mrs. Smith, *The Compleat Housewife* (London, 1727). The pages of the Preface are unnumbered; the passage begins on the sixth page on the recto side.

Ibid., Preface, the passage begins on the third page on the recto side.

Household Ordinances, pp. 440, 441.

Mrs. Smith, *The Compleat Housewife* (London, 1727), p. 13f.

are both mentioned by name, that great attention is now given to vegetables,* and that the preservation of food has become increasingly important. The medieval books of recipes occasionally include such subjects as 'to scour rust from venison', but the whole subject of preservation now receives much more attention, and various answers to the difficulty are proposed, which have been touched on in the Introduction.

Cookery books of the early eighteenth century are few in number; the next to concern us is *The Art of Cookery Made Plain and Easy*, published anonymously in 1747, and described on the title page as being 'By a Lady'. This was a fairly common subterfuge of the period; later editions give the author's name as 'H. Glasse' or 'Hannah Glasse'. There has been controversy about the person so described almost since the book was published; it seems to have died down about the end of the nineteenth century, and George Augustus Sala is the last writer of reputation to have engaged in it. It seems probable that the name 'Hannah Glasse' is a nom-de-plume for a hack writer named John Hill, though the name of Mrs. Glasse has remained attached to the book. As the title implies, this was a cookery book only, and apart from two pages at the end with cures for various illnesses, including Dr. Meade's cure, and remarks on the treatment both of plague and of bugs, no subjects other than cookery are included. The surprise of the book is a violent attack on French cooks, which opens with the following on page iv:

'You may leave out the Wine, according to what Use you want it for; so that really one might have a genteel Entertainment, for the Price the Sauce of one Dish comes to: But, if Gentlemen will have French Cooks, they must pay for French Tricks.
'A *Frenchman*, in his own Country, would dress a fine Dinner of twenty Dishes, and all genteel and pretty, for the Expence he will put an *English* Lord to for dressing one Dish. But there is the little petty Profit. I have heard of a Cook that used six Pounds of Butter to fry twelve Eggs; when every Body knows (that understands Cooking) that Half a Pound is full enough, or more than need be used: but then it would not be *French*. So much is the blind Folly of this Age, that they would rather be impos'd on by a *French* Booby, than give Encouragement to a good *English* Cook!'

This is repeated later '. . . It would be needless to name any more; though you have much more expensive Sauce than this. However I think here is enough to shew the Folly of these fine *French* Cooks. In their own Country, they will make a grand Entertainment with the Expence of one of these Dishes; but here they want the little petty Profit; and by this Sort of Legerdemain, some fine Estates are Juggled into *France*.'*

Hannah Glasse, *The Art of Cookery Made Plain and Easy* (London, 1747), p. 106.

Diary, August 28, 1783.

Parson Woodforde's *Diary* echoes this. He describes an elaborate dinner and then says 'Most of the things spoiled by being so Frenchified in dressing'.* This anti-French bias does not prevent the use of slightly anglicized French terms, such as 'a ragoo'.

Mrs. Glasse's book is in many ways similar to that of Mrs. Smith. It includes very medieval-sounding recipes such as that for cooking larks* as well as more modern ones, for instance those for rice pudding* and for tripe.* Sauce has a far greater importance than it would have had at an earlier date,* and though no French names are given, a number of the sauces are of recognizably French origin. Although the vessel containing sauce is commonly described as 'a cup', the sauce-boat is mentioned by name at least once.* Slices of fresh lemon as a garnish are recommended throughout the book.

Hannah Glasse, *op. cit.*, p. 96.
Ibid., p. 211.
Ibid., pp. 24, 25.
Ibid., p. 67f.

Ibid., p. 10.

In contrast to Mrs. Smith, the problem of preservation is treated here in the rather offhand medieval way, in a recipe 'To keep Venison or Hares sweet; or to make them fresh, when they stink'.* Of far more concern to Mrs. Glasse is the subject of Invalid Food,

Ibid., p. 10.

'*To make Beef or Mutton Broth*
Take a Pound of Beef, or Mutton, or both together: To a Pound put two
Quarts of Water, first skin the Meat and take off all the Fat; then cut it into
little Pieces, and boil it till it comes to a Quarter of a Pint. Season it with a
very little Corn of Salt, skim off all the Fat, and give a Spoonful of this
Broth at a Time. To very weak people, Half a Spoonful is enough; to some
a Tea Spoonful at a Time; and to other a Tea-cup full. There is greater
Nourishment from this than any Thing else.'*   *Ibid.*, pp. 233f.

Mrs. Glasse's interest here is a parallel to that of the Paris cooks which led
to the opening of the first restaurant, a subject which has been touched on
in the Introduction. Italy only appears in the recipe for Bologna sausages:

'*To make Bologna Sausages*
Take a Pound of Bacon, Fat and Lean together, a Pound of Beef, a Pound of
Veal, a Pound of Pork, a Pound of Beef Sewet, cut them small and chop
them fine, take a small Handful of Sage, pick off the Leaves, chop it fine,
with a few Sweet Herbs; season pretty high with Pepper and Salt. You must
have a large Gut, and fill it; then set on a Sauce-pan of Water, when it
boils put it in, and prick the Gut for fear of bursting. Boil it softly an Hour,
then lay it on clean Straw to dry.'*   *Ibid.*, p. 251.

On the other hand, anyone who has travelled in Germany will notice the
following with interest:

'*Suppe Mit Ei*
To make Buttered Water, or what the Germans call Egg-Soop, and are
very fond of it for Supper.
Take a Pint of Water, beat up the Yolk of an Egg with the Water, put in a
Piece of Butter as big as a small Walnut, two or three Nobs of Sugar, and
keep stiring it all the Time it is on the Fire. When it begins to boil, bruise it
between the Sauce-pan and a Mug till it is smooth, and has a great Froth;
then it is fit to drink. This is ordered in a Cold, or where Egg will agree
with the Stomach.'*   *Ibid.*, p. 238.

As with Mrs. Smith, considerable stress is laid on the cooking of vegetables,*   *Ibid.*, p. 15f.
while another note that appears in many eighteenth century cookery books
is the series of recipes for one dish to look like another. This is most clearly
represented here in the recipes for a chicken done up to look like a pheasant:

'. . . If you have but one Pheasant, take a large fine fowl about the Bigness of
a Pheasant, pick it nicely with the Head on, draw it and truss it with the
Head turn'd as you do a Pheasant's, lard the Fowl all over the Breast and
Legs with a large Piece of Bacon cut in little Pieces; when roasted put them
both in a Dish, and no Body will know it. They will take an Hour doing,
as the Fire must not be too brisk. A *Frenchman* would order Fish Sauce to
them, but then you quite spoil your Pheasants.'*   *Ibid.*, p. 93.

Another recipe of the same type, rather more surprising in its title, is headed
'To make an Egg as big as Twenty.'*   *Ibid.*, p. 201.
Mrs. Glasse, like Mrs. Smith, writes for the beginner rather than the
expert. There is a section on Marketing, and also notes on what is ripe at
what season in the vegetable and fruit garden.* At the very end of the book   *Ibid.*, p. 316f.
she includes a recipe for Ice Cream:

'Take two Pewter Basons, one larger than the other; the inward one must
have a close Cover, into which you are to put your Cream, and mix it with
Raspberries or whatever you like best, to give it a Flavour and a Colour.
Sweeten it to your Palate; then cover it close, and set it into the larger Bason.

Ibid., p. 332.

Fill it with Ice, and a Handful of Salt; let it stand in this Ice three Quarters of an Hour, then uncover it, and stir the Cream well together; cover it close again, and let it stand Half an Hour longer, after that turn it into your Plate. These Things are made at the Pewterers.'*

Although ice cream had been introduced by Charles II on his return from France, this seems to be its first appearance in an English cookery book.

Mrs. Smith and Mrs. Glasse had many successors. Dr. Johnson once said that he would write a cookery book 'on philosophical principles',* but there is no indication that he did so and it will be best to turn aside at this point to consider a quite new factor—the public appearance of the Epicure. This word has been dealt with above; in its modern meaning its use in English seems to date from the middle of the sixteenth century. Gourmet, which now has much the same meaning, dates only from 1820. The most famous of the epicure authors is Auguste Brillat-Savarin, whose *La Physiologie du Goût* appeared in 1825. A contemporary, also a doctor, who seems to have had some influence on Brillat-Savarin and whose book was published eight years earlier, was Dr. William Kitchiner, the author of *Apicius Redivivus, or The Cook's Oracle*, 1817. The Epicure, unlike the professional cook, writes essentially about the pleasures of eating and drinking, rather than concentrating on the preparation of food. Dr. Kitchiner is like the professional cook in including a large number of recipes, but unlike him in that he writes from the independent standpoint of a practising doctor, as Brillat-Savarin was to do. His book is also important in that exact details of the quantities of ingredients in any dish are given. In this it differs from books written at an earlier date, in which such points are not considered.

Boswell, *Life*; the conversation in which this occurred took place in April 1778 at Dilley's the bookseller's.

There have been innumerable followers in the path first taken by Kitchiner and Brillat-Savarin. The earliest ones of importance were Thomas Walker, whose 'Aristology' was published in 1835 in a magazine he edited, *The Original*, and Abraham Hayward, whose *The Art of Dining* appeared in 1851, though its material had appeared many years earlier.* There have been far too many writers on similar subjects since then for it to be possible even to consider mentioning them.

In 1835 and 1836 as reviews of the books by Brillat-Savarin and Walker appearing in the *Cornhill Magazine*.

The cookery books of the eighteenth century did not, in the main, survive the Napoleonic War, and the new generation seems to have turned elsewhere for information. Many new cookery books were published during the first part of the nineteenth century, and show to a marked degree the difference in attitude, both of author and reader, brought about by the new supremacy of the middle classes. One dating from the first decade of the nineteenth century, and consequently too early in date to show more than the beginnings of this difference—it was published sixty-two years after Mrs. Glasse—was *A New System of Domestic Cookery founded upon Principles of Economy. By a Lady*, 1807.* Like its predecessors, this has some characteristics that are old and some that are new. To the former class belong the remarks on Carving, and how it was shared between host, hostess and guest, as well as those on 'Cookery for the Sick and for the Poor'. As to the latter, we note that in contrast to earlier books, the recipes given for each kind of dish are now grouped together in separate Parts (for Soup, for Fish, for Meat, for Poultry, for Game, and so on.) Part IV is on Soups and Gravies, Part V on Sauces—both subjects were obviously far more important to the hostess of 1807 than they had been at an earlier date. Part VI is on Pies, Puddings and Pastry, Part VII on Vegetables, Part VIII on Sweet Dishes, Sweetmeats and Preserved Fruits, and Part IX on Cakes and Bread. The other sections of the book are dealt with elsewhere.

The 'Lady' is said to be Mrs. Maria Eliza Rundell. The book seems to be English in origin, but the editions after the first were published simultaneously in England and the U.S.A.

One of the really striking examples of this new nineteenth century attitude is Alexis Soyer's *The Gastronomic Regenerator*, 1848 (Plates 35 and 37), but what is perhaps the most important in the list of English cookery books is Mrs. Beeton's *Book of Household Management*, 1861. In the kind of information given and the classes it was obviously intended for this contrasts vividly with the eighteenth century books. The contrast is nowhere more clearly borne out than in the opening observations on luncheon (Mrs. Beeton always uses this form of the word), dinner, evening parties and evenings without parties, as well as on the mistress in general. Little space, however, is devoted to any of these subjects except dinner, and we are soon in the middle of the familiar list of what is in season at which times of the year, now under the separate headings of fish, meat, game, poultry, vegetables and fruit.* The subject of preservation receives a number of general remarks and is in the author's mind throughout the book. It is clear that by 1861 it had begun to receive the serious attention that it does today.* The presence of a Glossary of French terms (though these had been used indiscriminately by eighteenth century writers) is a further mark of the new age.*

Mrs. Beeton, *Book of Household Management*, 1869, p. 37f.

Ibid., p. 51.

Ibid., p. 46.

When we turn to the recipes which immediately follow this opening section, we see that each subject receives two chapters, one containing general observations, the other the recipes. The book is as large as it is partly because more subjects are covered in it than in its predecessors, and partly because greater detail involves more recipes. The recipes are now arranged in alphabetical order, and each one lists the ingredients, the mode of preparation, the time taken, the cost, the time of year at which the dish is seasonable, and the number of people served. Each recipe for fish is embellished with a small woodcut of the fish. In the matter of the comparative number of recipes for fish, we may observe that there are five for eels, six for oysters, in a note to one of which Mrs. Beeton puts the French firmly in their place on the subject of the origin of the oyster:

'The French assert that the English oysters, which are esteemed the best in Europe, were originally procured from Cancalle Bay, near St. Malo; but they assign no proof for this. It is a fact, however, that the oysters eaten in ancient Rome were nourished in the channel which then parted the Isle of Thanet from England, and which has since been filled up, and converted into meadows.'*

Ibid., p. 150, recipe 300.

There are then seven recipes for salmon, but nine for sole, seemingly now the most popular fish. Sturgeon and sterlet are both mentioned, but there is no reference to caviar, although this had been known in England since the sixteenth century, and is referred to in Shakespeare's *Hamlet* II. ii. Eight pounds of it were ordered for the Garter meeting at Windsor in 1670,* but later references are not common. Fish is followed, and the meats preceded, by two chapters on sauces, gravies, force meats and pickles. The general chapter opens with the story of the Duc de Soubise, the Chef and the hams:

Christopher Hibbert, *The Court at Windsor* (London, 1964), p. 79.

'An anecdote is told of the Prince de Soubise, who, intending to give an entertainment, asked for the bill of fare. His *chef* came, presenting a list adorned with vignettes, and the first article of which, that met the prince's eye, was "fifty hams". "Bertrand," said the prince, "I think you must be extravagant. Fifty hams! do you intend to feast my whole regiment?" "No, Prince, there will be but one on the table, and the surplus I need for my Espagnole, blondes, garnitures etc." "Bertrand, you are robbing me: this item will not do." "Monseigneur," said the *artiste*, "you do not appreciate me. Give me the order, and I will put those fifty hams in a crystal flask no bigger than my thumb." The prince smiled, and the hams were passed.'*

Mrs. Beeton, *Book of Household Management*, 1869, p. 182.

Mrs. Beeton goes on to consider the all-embracing importance of sauces.

Two chapters are then devoted to beef, two to mutton and lamb, and two to pork; the general one in each case begins with a short discussion of the various species of the animal, and ends with a section on carving, important because it seems to imply that the carver would have no previous knowledge of the animal's anatomy. The second contains the recipes, many of them accompanied by notes which generally, though not always, have a close connection with the recipe. An example is the note accompanying Recipe 453:

'*Venison*: Far, far away in ages past, our fathers loved the chase, and what it brought; and it is usually imagined that when Isaac ordered his son Esau to go out with his weapons, his quiver and his bow, and to prepare for him savoury meat, such as he loved, that it was venison he desired. The wise Solomon, too, delighted in this kind of fare; for we learn that, at his table, every day were served the wild ox, the roebuck, and the stag. Xenophon informs us, in his History, that Cyrus, King of Persia, ordered that venison should never be wanting at his repasts; and of the effeminate Greeks it was the delight. The Romans, also, were devoted admirers of the flesh of the deer; and our own kings and princes, from the Great Alfred down to the late Prince Consort, have hunted, although, it must be confessed, under vastly different circumstances, the swift buck, and relished their "haunch" all the more keenly, that they had borne themselves bravely in the pursuit of the animal.'

These are given in even smaller type than the rest of the book and make us put it down with a high respect for Victorian eyes as well as for Victorian stomachs.

The pork chapter is important as containing what seems to be the first mention of the modern breakfast dish *par excellence*—bacon and eggs. In all the early editions there are recipes for fried bacon and poached eggs (not specifically called *a breakfast dish*), and for broiled rashers of bacon, called *a breakfast dish*. Breakfast, indeed, plays a large part, and there are many recipes marked either *A Breakfast or Luncheon Dish* or even, in one case, *A Breakfast, Luncheon or Supper Dish*. Here, indeed, we meet the most important of the Victorian contributions to our subject. Eighteenth century breakfasts were light; it is with Mrs. Beeton that we meet the full-scale meal of the modern kind. After pork the book proceeds first to veal, then to poultry and then to game. The poultry chapter contains a note and an illustration, though no recipes, for a cygnet, and the following note on the turkey,

Ibid., p. 504.

'The common turkey is a native of North America, and, in the reign of Henry VIII, was introduced into England. According to Tusser's "Five Hundred Points of Good Husbandry", it began about the year 1585 to form a dish at our rural Christmas feasts:-
   "Beefe, mutton, and pork, shred pies of the best,
      Pig, veal, goose, and capon, and turkey well drest;
      Cheese, apples, and nuts, jolly carols to hear,
      As then in the country is counted good cheer".'*

The recipes for game are chiefly notable for a scope much wider than any earlier book. Ptarmigan, teal and 'landrail or corncrake' are all included. These chapters conclude with one on vegetables, of which twenty-seven are mentioned, two or three recipes for each being the average; some, such as potatoes receive far more.

After this we find Desserts, Egg Dishes, Cakes and Beverages. The most interesting features of the chapters on desserts are the references to ice cream. Mrs. Glasse's single reference to the subject has already been noted. It is now regarded as a normal thing; a plea is made for Catherine de'Medici, with the facetious suggestion that the advantages brought by ice cream eating more than make up for the Massacre of St. Bartholomew's Eve,* and there are recipes for ice puddings and notes on the ice-making machine. The eighteenth century almond dish known as a 'Hedgehog' appears again by name,* and the medieval 'Daryole', mentioned above on page 53, is found again in a recipe:

Ibid., p. 782.

Ibid., p. 719.

'*Darioles à la Vanille* (*Sweet Entremêts*)
Ingredients:- ½ pint of milk, ½ pint of cream, 2 ozs. of flour, 3 ozs. of pounded sugar, 6 eggs, 2 ozs. of butter, puff-paste, flavouring of essence of vanilla. *Mode:-* Mix the flour to a smooth batter with the milk; stir in the cream, sugar, the eggs, which should be well whisked, and the butter, which should be beaten to a cream. Put in some essence of vanilla, drop by drop, until the mixture is well flavoured; line some dariole moulds with puff-paste, three-parts fill them with the batter, and bake in a good oven from 25 to 35 minutes. Turn them out of the moulds on a dish, without breaking them; strew over sifted sugar, and serve. The flavouring of the darioles may be varied by substituting lemon, cinnamon, or almonds, for the vanilla. *Time:-* 25 to 35 minutes. Average cost, 1s. 8d. Sufficient to fill 6 or 7 dariole-moulds. Seasonable at any time.'*

Ibid., p. 739.

In contrast to this medieval touch, omelettes, pancakes, rice, sago, semolina and tapioca all appear, as does a curious and otherwise unknown adaptation of the familiar *blanc mange*, called '*Jaune Mange*'.* (The word *blanc mange*, sometimes spelled *blamange*, is medieval in origin, but until the eighteenth century referred to the white meat of chickens and other birds; only then does it appear to have acquired its modern meaning).

Ibid., p. 745.

Of the other chapters only that on beverages requires mention. Tea and coffee both appear, though there is no reference to the drinking of chocolate; the section on tea contains a description of the 'Tea Float', the ancestor of that unpleasant modern institution, the 'Tea Bag'.* As to the alcoholic drinks, it is surprising to discover that the middle Victorians considered Port Negus a drink for children.

Ibid., p. 917.

'*To make negus.* Ingredients:- To every pint of port wine allow 1 quart of boiling water, ¼ lb of sugar, 1 lemon, grated nutmeg to taste. *Mode:-* As this beverage is more usually drunk at children's parties than at any other, the wine need not be very old or expensive for the purpose, a new fruity wine answering very well for it. Put the wine into a jug, rub some lumps of sugar (equal to ¼ lb) on the lemon rind until all the yellow part of the skin is absorbed, then squeeze the juice, and strain it. Add the sugar and lemon-juice to the port wine ,with the grated nutmeg; pour over it the boiling water, cover the jug, and, when the beverage has cooled a little, it will be fit for use. Negus may also be made of sherry, or any other sweet white wine, but is more usually made of port than of any other beverage. *Sufficient.* Allow 1 pint of wine, with the other ingredients in proportion, for a party of 9 or 10 children.'*

Ibid., p. 929.

The later chapters of the section on food are considered elsewhere. The remainder of the book is concerned with the Household rather than the Kitchen or the Dining Room.